W9-BZB-604

Altar Guild
and Sacristy
Handbook

ALTAR GUILD
AND SACRISTY
HANDBOOK

S. Anita Stauffer

AUGSBURG FORTRESS / MINNEAPOLIS

Altar Guild and Sacristy Handbook
Copyright © 2000 Augsburg Fortress. All rights reserved. Except brief quotations in critical articles or reviews, no part of this book may be reproduced in any manner without prior written permission from the publisher. Write to: Permissions, Augsburg Fortress, Box 1209, Minneapolis, MN 55440-1209.

Scripture quotations, unless otherwise noted, are from the New Revised Standard Version (NRSV) Bible, copyright © 1989 Division of Christian Education of the National Council of the Churches of Christ in the United States of America. Used by permission.

Prayers and liturgical texts acknowledged as *LBW* are from *Lutheran Book of Worship*, copyright © 1978, administered by Augsburg Fortress, and those acknowledged as *Occasional Services* are copyright © 1982, administered by Augsburg Fortress.

Book design: Richard Krogstad
Cover and interior art: Jane Pitz
Editors: Dennis Bushkofsky, Rebecca Lowe

Library of Congress Cataloging-in-Publication Data
Stauffer, S. Anita.
    Altar guild and sacristy handbook / S. Anita Stauffer.
      p. cm.
    Includes bibliographical references (p. 130) and index.
    ISBN 0-8066-3896-6 (alk. paper)
      1. Altar guilds—Lutheran Church—Handbooks, manuals, etc. 2. Sacristans—
    Handbooks, manuals, etc. 1. Title.
    BX8067.A77.S73 2000
    247'.088'241—dc21   00-038945

Manufactured in the U.S.A.   ISBN 0-8066-3896-6   AFP 3-1760
07 06 05 04 03 02 01 00   3 4 5 6 7 8 9 10

IN HONOR OF AND THANKSGIVING FOR

The ones who first taught me the reality of love –
my parents, Betty (R.I.P.) and Laverne Stauffer

The one whose life and teaching
first proved to me the living reality of God –
Robert J. Esbjornson

And the many who have taught me so much
about the worship of this God, most especially –
R. R. Van Loon
Eugene L. Brand
Gordon W. Lathrop
Anscar J. Chupungco, OSB

CONTENTS

1. MINISTRY

. . . Be filled with the Spirit, as you sing psalms and h
songs among yourselves, singing and making melody to
hearts, giving thanks to God the Father at all times and for e
name of our Lord Jesus Christ.
– (Ephesians 5:18-20)

Before one is an altar guild member or sacristan in one's congre
tion, one is a baptized, worshiping, communing Christian. Th
fact prompts a certain attitude in one's heart: the attitude of thanksgiving to God in the name of our Lord Jesus. That attitude, in turn,
prompts how one serves in the altar guild. Serving in an altar guild or as
a sacristan is not like participating in social groups in parishes, for the
altar guild is a *ministry*. Indeed, it is a ministry that can only be carried
out with a song in one's heart. Why?

When you were installed as a member of the altar guild, you were
probably addressed with these or similar words:

> Dear Christian friends: Baptized into the priesthood of Christ, we are called
> to offer ourselves to the Lord of the Church for what he has done and con-
> tinues to do for us.
> – *(Occasional Services)*

These words point to our motivation for serving in the guild. What
has Christ done for us? He died to take away our sin. He rose from the
grave to defeat the power of death. Christ has given us new life by joining us to his own death and resurrection in our baptism. What does he
continue to do for us? Christ renews in us the power of forgiveness. He
gives us hope and joy in the proclamation of the gospel. He gives us love
and support in the human communion (or fellowship) of the church. He
gives us the bread of life and the cup of blessing in the Holy Communion
(or *eucharist*). Christ's Spirit fills us with songs of thanksgiving for all that
God has done for us. In response to all of this, and to all of God's other
mighty acts, we are called to offer ourselves to Christ's service. The basic
motivation for serving in the altar guild or as a sacristan is gratitude.

Members of the altar guild are grateful servants: ministers of God, ministers of God's people, ministers of the liturgy, and ministers of the worship space.

MINISTERS OF GOD

Joy is the cardinal attribute of the ministers of God. This attribute is not the same thing as happiness. Rather, this is the immeasurably deep joy of our deliverance from sin and death, the great joy of Christ's incarnation and resurrection. It is the joy of our baptism, the joy of the gospel, the joy of the eucharist. Joy stems from our gratitude for all that God has done and is doing for us. More basically, joy is a natural response to God's presence. The joy of these realities enables work in the altar guild to be carried out with a sense of privilege. Whether it is preparing the altar, polishing vessels, removing wax from a linen, arranging flowers, or pressing vestments, the work is never a burden but is always a privilege. It is *ministry*—which we do as a form of praise and an expression of joy. Our praise is simply because God is God. As the ancient *Te Deum* puts it: "You are God; we praise you. You are the Lord; we acclaim you."

The sense of joy, praise, and privilege is joined to that of reverence. Reverence is a deep sense of awe and mystery and wonder and ultimate respect in the presence of the Holy One. Our reverence is expressed in the way we think and feel and speak and act, in how we handle the things of worship and care for the altar, in our attitude toward our fellow ministers of the liturgy, and in our own worship and prayer.

Because the altar represents God's presence, it is fitting that we act and speak reverently whenever we are in the worship space. Whether there on Saturday preparing the altar, or on Sunday worshiping with the congregation, conduct should express our devotion to God. When entering the worship space to carry out altar guild responsibilities, it is helpful to pray that the work may be done to the glory of God, and that the tasks may be seen as an opportunity to serve God. A life of prayer is a good and fitting foundation for the work of the altar guild/sacristans.

Prayer is also an appropriate accompaniment to the actual work of altar guild members. To help become patterned in such prayer, some of the following, adapted from *Lutheran Book of Worship*, may be useful in one's personal prayer life. (Other prayers, for meetings, are provided in chapter 10.)

Heavenly Father, in whom we live and move and have our being, we humbly pray you so to guide and govern us by your Holy Spirit, that in all the cares and occupations of our life we may not forget you, but remember that we are ever walking in your sight; through Jesus Christ our Lord. Amen

Lord God of our salvation, it is your will that all people might come to you through your Son Jesus Christ. Inspire our witness to him, that all may know the power of his forgiveness and the hope of his resurrection. In Jesus' name. Amen

Almighty God, grant that we, who have been redeemed from the old life of sin by our baptism into the death and resurrection of your Son Jesus Christ, may be renewed in your Holy Spirit to live in righteousness and true holiness; through Jesus Christ our Lord. Amen

Almighty God, draw our hearts to you, guide our minds, fill our imaginations, control our wills, so that we may be wholly yours. Use us as you will, always to your glory and the welfare of your people; through our Lord and Savior Jesus Christ. Amen

Bless us, O God, with a reverent sense of your presence, that we may be at peace and may worship and serve you with all our mind and spirit; through Jesus Christ our Lord. Amen

Direct us, O Lord, in all our doings with your most gracious favor and further us with your continual help, that in all our works, begun, continued, and ended in you, we may glorify your holy name and finally, by your mercy, obtain everlasting life; through Jesus Christ our Lord. Amen

We express our joy, reverence, and identity as baptized Christians in various actions and words. Just as God embodied God's grace in Jesus, God also made us embodied creatures. We are made of flesh and blood, and God gave us five senses. God relates to us—and we relate to God—in actions as well as words.

Certain actions are filled with meaning for Christians. They symbolize our reverence and our faith; they are enacted prayer. We stand in worship to give honor to the risen Christ who is in our midst. We kneel to express our humility in the presence of God.

Making the sign of the cross is an action that reminds us of our baptism. Since at least the second century, Christians have made the sign of the cross as a remembrance that in Holy Baptism, God makes us Christ's own children forever. The sign of the cross is a symbol of our salvation, a reminder that on the cross, Christ has consecrated our whole selves—minds, hearts, and actions. (The thumb and/or fingers are touched briefly on the forehead, then the chest, then the left shoulder and right shoulder, and finally on the chest once again.)

Bowing is also an action of reverence. We may bow our heads in prayer to show our respect for God. We may bow toward the cross with our heads or from the waist as it is carried in procession, because it represents Christ's presence among us. Many Christians bow their heads when the name of Jesus Christ is mentioned in liturgy, as a sign that we accept him as Lord: ". . . At the name of Jesus every knee should bend, in heaven and on earth and under the earth, and every tongue should confess that Jesus Christ is Lord, to the glory of God the Father" (Philippians 2:10-11).

Such ritual actions help us embody our faith. They stimulate worshipful and prayerful attitudes. They are a means of expressing and reinforcing our reverence and adoration for the holiness of God. These outward signs of devotion are acceptable to God, for they flow out of hearts full of love for God and obedience to God's will. The way we live our lives affects how we serve in the altar guild: "Who can ascend the hill of the Lord and who can stand in his holy place? Those who have clean hands and a pure heart, who have not pledged themselves to falsehood, nor sworn by what is a fraud" (Psalm 24:3-4; *LBW*). The inner life of prayer and the corporate life of worship—with lament, confession of sinfulness, praise and adoration of God solely because God is God, thanksgiving for all that God has done for us, petitions for God's help, intercessions for the needs of others, attentive listening to the word, and faithful sharing in the Lord's supper—are essential for those who serve God in the altar guild.

MINISTERS OF GOD'S PEOPLE

The church's liturgy is a public event. Corporate worship has both a vertical dimension (involving the worshiper with God) and a horizontal dimension (involving worshipers with each other). Altar guild members and sacristans are ministers of God's people as well as ministers of God. This means that guild members will be sensitive to how their work affects other people in the congregation.

People learn about God in part from how God is worshiped. Each thing that is done in worship (including tasks done by the altar guild/sacristans) teaches the congregation. The key question is whether what is taught is consistent with the church's theology. If the altar linens and paraments are kept spotless and the eucharistic vessels are beautiful, the congregation learns something of our respect for God. On the other hand, if soiled or wrinkled linens are used, the people may conclude that God is not important enough for careful preparations. It is important for altar guild members to remind themselves continually of the meaning and impact of what they do.

Another responsibility of altar guild members/sacristans to the congregation is reliability. Corporate worship involves the ministry of many—altar guild, presiding and assisting ministers, musicians, acolytes, ushers—and it is vital that each person fulfill his or her responsibility. The congregation relies on each person to be present and to have fulfilled his/her responsibility on each assigned Sunday or other day. This is ministry.

MINISTERS OF THE LITURGY

The liturgy is the church's form of corporate worship. The Sunday liturgy of word and sacrament has come to us from our ancestors in the faith, both Jewish and Christian. We use a liturgy derived in part from the ancient synagogue service, consisting of readings, psalms, prayers, and a type of sermon. The other part of our liturgy derives from the upper room, when Jesus identified the bread and wine of the Jewish ritual meal as his body and blood and said, "Do this for the remembrance of me." Since Pentecost, Christians have had an insatiable appetite for this meal, because in it Christ himself is present. We gather for word and sacrament because that is what our Lord told us to do. We use a liturgy that has come down to us through the ages because it sets us within the mainstream of Christian worship. This liturgy, from synagogue and Last supper, helps us remember and celebrate God's mighty acts of salvation.

Members of the altar guild are ministers of the liturgy. This ministry involves preparing the worship space with the furnishings, appointments, vessels, elements, linens, and paraments used in the liturgy. As these items are prepared and cared for, it is important that the altar guild understand their meaning and use in worship. Ongoing study is essential. (See chapter 10 for study suggestions.)

Ministers of the Worship Space

Altar guild members are also ministers of the worship space. Church buildings have been understood in two—often conflicting—ways. In past decades, the church has often been understood as the house of God, and persons often point to Jacob's words, "This is none other than the house of God, and this is the gate of heaven" (Genesis 28:17). In contrast, the original understanding of the church building was as the house of God's *people*. The building is the "house of the church," that is, the house of the people who through baptism comprise the church. This early Christian understanding is now being recovered.

The worship space, however, is actually a synthesis or combination of these two concepts. The building is the place of assembly, the place where God's baptized people gather to worship: for the baptismal bath, for the proclamation of the word, and for the sharing in the eucharistic meal. It is a witness to the corporate nature of the church. The building is also the *place of encounter*. It is the place where, more intensively than any other place in the world, we encounter the God whose we are; it is also the place where we encounter each other as baptized members of the body of Christ.

Who Are these Ministers?

This book uses the terms *altar guild members* and *sacristans* as synonyms. Traditionally, Lutherans have favored the term *altar guild,* but increasingly are also using the word *sacristan*. Different congregations use different words. Neither is better than the other; it is a matter of local preference. If there is an effort to enlist men to serve in this ministry, however, the term *sacristans* may be less intimidating to men simply because for Lutherans it is a newer term and does not carry the connotation that only women are wanted.

In ecumenical usage, *sacristan* is historically the more traditional word. In fact, in the ancient church, the preparation of the altar was a function reserved for men appointed or ordained to this ministry of liturgical preparations.

2. PLACES

Ascribe to the LORD the glory of his name;
worship the LORD in holy splendor.
–(Psalm 29:2)

Blessed are you, O Lord our God....We are the temple of your presence,
and this building is the house of your Church. Accept us and this place to
which we come to share with others the covenant you make through Holy
Baptism, to praise your name, to receive your forgiveness, to hear your
Word, and to be nourished by the body and blood of your Son.
–(Dedication of a Church, *Occasional Services*)

For nearly two thousand years, God's baptized people have gathered
each Sunday morning to worship—to acknowledge that God is the
Holy One, and to offer praise and acclamation: "You are God; we praise
you" *(Te Deum)*. We gather to worship in order to adore our Creator
and Redeemer and Sanctifier. We worship God simply because God is
God, because therefore God is worthy of being praised.

Worship is our adoring response to the Holy One whom we call
God. Worship is our encounter with this God—and with each other in
God's presence. Worship is the central and unique function of the
church; without worship, there would be no church. Worship identifies
the church *as* the church, for it is the one unique function of the church.

To worship, the baptized community assembles with awe in the presence of the Almighty. To worship is to remember the incarnation of our
Lord and to sing with the angels, "Glory to God in the highest!" It is to
recall the crucifixion and resurrection and to sing with the myriad saints
and angels at the heavenly banquet, "Worthy is Christ, the Lamb who
was slain." It is to stand in the awesome presence of God and to sing,
"Holy, holy, holy Lord, God of power and might: heaven and earth are
full of your glory." It is to be renewed and nourished with Christ's body
and blood and to sing with thanksgiving, "Lord, now you let your servant go in peace; your word has been fulfilled."

In corporate worship we celebrate the saving acts of God—in creation, in history, and in our own lives. We gather to remember and give thanks for all that God has done for God's people through the ages. We assemble in God's presence, we acknowledge God's holiness, we remember God's mighty acts of salvation, we praise and adore our Lord, and we are nourished by word and sacrament—this is Christian worship. We who are baptized gather each week to give thanks to God and to celebrate the presence and power of God's Son in our midst.

In worship we *are* the church. In worship we remember who we are: God's baptized family. In worship we find our identity, our peace, our healing, our forgiveness, our meaning, and our mission. Worship is both central to our individual lives as Christians, and central also to the life of the whole church throughout the world, across time and space and ecumenical divisions.

Christianity is a corporate faith; it is not a private affair between "God and me." We are the *corpus* or body of Christ. We are baptized into this body of Christ, the family of God, the whole church of every time and every place. Because in baptism we are joined to God's people, we gather with others in the body of Christ in local congregations on Sundays to worship, to pray, to hear the word, and to share in the eucharist.

Gathering a group for worship requires a *place* to gather, and since Old Testament times people have built beautiful buildings to honor God. Almost three thousand years ago, the temple in Jerusalem was dedicated by Solomon. The temple was a place of such splendor that it immediately captured the eye and aroused devotion. The Bible gives exact details of the beauty of the temple. The entire interior was overlaid with pure gold. The doors were carved with cherubim, palm trees, and flowers, and overlaid with gold. A pair of cherubim sixteen feet high, overlaid in gold, were in the Holy of Holies. The temple contained many silver, gold, and bronze lampstands, altars and other furnishings. It was a place of incredible magnificence.

The earliest Christians did not gather for worship in such magnificence. Being a Christian at that time was frequently viewed as a crime. Christians were often under persecution, and discovery led to imprisonment and even death. Christians usually had to worship in secret, and they most often gathered in private homes. That all changed, however, in 313 A.D., when the Roman emperor Constantine declared Christianity a legal religion and brought an end to the persecution. Since then,

Christians have built and dedicated special places for worship. Like the temple in the Old Testament, the early Christian church buildings were often places of great beauty, filled with gold and mosaics and marble. As the number of Christians increased, the need for larger church buildings arose. By the Middle Ages, huge Romanesque and Gothic church buildings were erected across Europe with magnificent stained glass windows, rich sculpture, mosaics, and other art depicting Christ and angels and saints and biblical scenes.

Church buildings are meeting places between God and God's people, and thus are places of both mystery and hospitality. While always and everywhere present, the triune God is present most fully and most powerfully in worship. Worship is the time when we come into God's presence most intentionally and most intensively. Through their architecture, beauty, and symbolism, church buildings help us to be most fully present to God. Surrounded by reminders of God's awesome and redeeming presence, we worship God, we give God thanks, and we praise God for the divine glory.

Church buildings are places for the people of God to gather for worship, places in which the gospel is proclaimed through word and sacrament, places for bringing life and hope to God's people and to the world. The final prayer for dedicating a church building makes clear the purposes:

> Blessed are you, O Lord our God, king of the universe. The heavens and the earth cannot contain you, yet you are willing to make your home in human hearts. We are the temple of your presence, and this building is the house of your Church. Accept us and this place to which we come to share with others the covenant you make through Holy Baptism, to praise your name, to receive your forgiveness, to hear your Word, and to be nourished by the body and blood of your Son. Be present always to guide and illumine your people. And now, O God, visit us with your mercy and blessing as we dedicate this house to your glory and honor and to the service of all people in the name of the Father, and of the Son, and of the Holy Spirit. Amen
> —(*Occasional Services*)

It is the privilege of the altar guild and sacristans to help care for this unique place built and dedicated to the honor, mystery, and glory of God and for hospitality to the people of God.

Before considering the specifics of the worship space and its sections and various appointments, it is fitting to consider overall guidelines, including beauty, simplicity, quality, worthiness, appropriateness, and cultural relevance.

BEAUTY Since Old Testament times, people have associated beauty with the worship of God: "Worship the LORD in the beauty of holiness" (Psalm 29:2, *LBW*). Beauty helps set awe and wonder as the context for liturgy. The altar guild has an important responsibility in making the worship space beautiful. Attention is given to the beauty of worship furnishings—beauty in the materials used, their design and form, their color and texture. Another aspect of beauty is harmony—how the various furnishings relate to each other and to the worship space as a whole. Beauty is often defined differently in different cultural contexts (see below).

SIMPLICITY Noble simplicity is an important part of beauty in many cultural contexts. The worship space should enable persons' eyes to focus easily and naturally on the central things: altar, baptismal font/pool, and pulpit/ambo. Too many banners, too many flowers and other items make a cluttered space, create visual pollution, and distract worshipers from the central things.

QUALITY Quality involves authenticity, as well as the care and skill with which things are made. Phoniness has no place in worship. Everything that is artificial or shoddy or of poor quality should be avoided. It is better, for example, to have no flowers at all than to have artificial flowers. Artificial flowers are not real; they are not a part of God's creation. Because they are fake, they simply cannot communicate the beauty of creation. Quality does not mean high cost, but honesty of materials. Everything in the worship space should actually and genuinely be what it appears to be. Anything which is counterfeit, bogus, or artificial should be avoided because it lacks the quality of truth. We are called by Jesus to "worship in spirit and in truth" (John 4:24).

WORTHINESS Worthiness is related to quality. All of the furnishings of the worship space should be worthy of the God whom we worship. They should be the best that the congregation can provide, and they should be cared for well. Soiled linens and wrinkled vestments are not worthy of God or of the worshiping assembly. The vessels, vestments, paraments, and ornaments of worship should point to the mystery of God; this does not necessarily mean great expense.

Likewise, though we live in a disposable culture, the disposable has no place in Christian worship. For example, small disposable paper or plastic communion glasses are not of a quality worthy of what they hold: the blood of Christ, shed on the cross for our salvation.

APPROPRIATENESS   Things used in worship should be appropriate both to the time of the liturgical year and to the service being used. The worship space should look quite different on a Sunday of Easter from a Sunday in Advent. Likewise, it should be different for Holy Communion than for Evening Prayer. Things are appropriate when they serve the liturgy; they are inappropriate when they are not in accord with the church's theology and tradition. In all cases, the central things remain central: baptismal font/pool, altar, pulpit/ambo—but the other appointments change, often seasonally and sometimes according to cultural context.

CULTURAL RELEVANCE   Worship appointments may represent the cultural context of the congregation. For example, one would not rightly expect certain appointments and decorations to look the same in a American Indian congregation, a Swedish American congregation, an African American congregation, a Chinese American congregation, a French Canadian parish, and a Slovak American congregation. While the central things are there in all cases, their design may be reflective of the congregation's ethnic heritage and local context.

Whether or not we realize it, parish worship always takes place in local context, and Christianity both affirms and corrects—says "yes" and "no"—to the culture surrounding local congregations. Our cultural setting shapes the ways in which we live and think, work and play. It shapes our worship one way or another, for it reflects the ethnic background and cultural context of the baptized in *this* particular place. Essentially, Christian worship relates to culture in four ways.

Worship is *contextual,* reflective of and varying with the local natural and cultural settings. Our Lord was born in a particular context, and his incarnation is the model and mandate for cultural relevance (also known as contextualization). Flowers and the design of paraments, vestments, and liturgical vessels and appointments appropriately vary between urban and rural, seaside and plains and mountainous settings—as well as between those in the cold northern climate and the temperate southern climate of North America. Multicultural congregations will reflect at various times and in various ways the variety of the members' cultural backgrounds.

Worship is *cross-cultural,* making sharing across cultures possible. Such sharing is most obvious in hymns and church music, though it may be reflected in art and other ways as well. Jesus is the savior of all people, and cross-cultural sharing is one means of manifesting our baptismal unity in Christ. However, there is a caution needed here: tokenism and eclecticism should be avoided. Music, art, and other elements from different cultures must be understood and respected before they are used in Christian worship, so that they are not trivialized.

Worship is *transcultural*—the same substance (word and sacrament) for everyone everywhere. In the use of the historic creeds, or the Lord's Prayer, or the Bible readings and psalms, for example, our worship is beyond our own local culture. The Christ into whom we are baptized is beyond us; Christ transcends all cultures, all races, all human divisions. Our congregations may be culturally and/or ethnically diverse, but they are all centered on the one Lord Jesus Christ; it is Christ alone whom we worship.

Worship is also *counter-cultural,* resisting and challenging anything in a given local culture that is contrary to the gospel of Jesus Christ. Local cultural practices and forms are critiqued when they are contradictory to the gospel; they must be transformed in order to be used in Christian worship. Christians observe Advent as a time of waiting and preparing, even as the world puts up Christmas decorations and plays Christmas carols in malls in the autumn. Christians also come to participate actively in the liturgy—not to be entertained passively, as they are in some other elements of North American culture.

Together, these four principles of worship's relationship to culture reflect the necessary balance between the local and the global. In doing so, the principles provide background guidance for many decisions that must be made by altar guilds, sacristans, and worship planners and committees. The *style* of worship (the genre of preaching, the music and hymns, and the visual environment of the worship space) may vary from congregation to congregation—worship is contextual—but the *content* of worship (Christ incarnate, crucified, risen and ascended), and the essential *shape* of worship (gathering, word of God, eucharistic meal, and sending out for mission) are the same around the globe—worship is transcultural. Some specific implications related to cultural setting are noted in other parts of this book.

WORSHIP SPACE AND ITS APPOINTMENTS

The altar guild is responsible for preparing the physical settings for the corporate liturgical life of the congregation. The space used for corporate worship is called the worship space. Church buildings usually have three main divisions of worship space: narthex, nave, and chancel (with the sacristies as preparatory liturgical spaces). In many newer buildings, there is less distinction between nave and chancel, though the chancel (even if it is in the center of the space) is still usually raised for the purpose of visibility. It is helpful for members of the altar guild to be familiar with the correct terminology for worship space and its furnishings and appointments.

Narthex

The narthex is the place of gathering and entering, the place of transition from everyday life as individuals and families to corporate worship with the baptized people of God. It is a place for persons to greet one another and to prepare for worship. The narthex also has important liturgical functions. It is used for the formation of liturgical processions prior to the entrance hymn in the eucharistic liturgy, wedding processions, and the burial procession prior to the funeral rite. In addition, the congregation as a whole may gather in or move in procession through the narthex on such days as the Sunday of the Passion (Palm Sunday), Easter Eve, and the Day of Pentecost. Receiving lines after weddings and other services also often form in the narthex.

As a place of entrance, transition, and preparation, the narthex (also known as the gathering space) should be an inviting and hospitable place that makes members and visitors feel welcome. It should be kept clean and uncluttered at all times.

Various pieces of art—such as sculpture, wall hangings, and paintings—may be placed in the narthex to reflect the day or season of the church year. Such art can help worshipers with the transition from the "outside" world to the place, event, and meaning of corporate worship.

Nave

The nave is the place of assembly, where the congregation gathers for worship. Derived from the Latin word *navis,* which means ship, the nave reminds us of the church sailing in the ocean of time; it is also a good baptismal reminder.

Traditionally in the West, the nave has been rectangular—long and relatively narrow, with the chancel at its head. Gradually, this arrangement has been replaced by more central spaces—square, round, octagonal, or hexagonal, for example. The central plan allows worshipers to feel more like participants (which they are by definition) than spectators. Some cultures are accustomed to central-plan spaces for sacred functions; this is particularly and traditionally true in Africa and for American Indians, thus making the central plan especially appropriate for African American and Native American congregations.

For many centuries baptismal fonts were located at the front of the nave (or even in the chancel), but the earlier tradition was at the rear of the nave. Today, it is most appropriate to place the baptismal space at the rear of the center aisle (see chapter 5).

Congregations are increasingly using chairs rather than pews in the nave, because of the flexibility in seating arrangements that chairs provide. Whether chairs or pews, it is helpful if they have kneelers. It is also useful if they have racks for worship books.

Space in the nave needs to be provided for disabled persons—seating that is easily entered and exited, as well as open space for wheelchairs. Quick and easy access to restrooms is crucial for persons with certain chronic illnesses as well as for parents with young children.

The aisles are as important as the seats. Aisles have three main functions. First, they allow the people to enter and be seated in the nave. Second, they allow the worshipers to access the altar for the distribution of Holy Communion, for corporate healing rites, and so forth. Third, they are the place of processions—entrance processions, gospel processions, offertory processions, wedding processions, burial processions, the procession of light in Evening Prayer, the procession with palms on the Sunday of the Passion, and the procession of the paschal candle at the Easter Vigil. Aisles should be wide enough for easy and safe movement in all of these uses, and for persons who must use crutches, wheelchairs, walkers, or other assisting devices.

Chancel

The third main section of worship space is the chancel—a raised platform in the front of the nave or near the middle of a centralized space. Most worship leadership is conducted from the chancel, since it is the place of both altar and pulpit/ambo.

In much traditional architecture, the chancel is composed of two parts: the sanctuary and the choir. The sanctuary is the area immediately surrounding the altar and is usually raised above the level of the rest of the chancel. This highest platform is known as the predella. (The term *sanctuary* is often used erroneously to refer to the entire worship space of a church, but this incorrect usage should be avoided for clarity, especially in ecumenical contexts.) In traditional architecture, the choir was the remaining area of the chancel, but the term has become much less useful since the singers are now often seated elsewhere than in the chancel.

The most central furnishing of the chancel is the altar, the table of the Lord. The pulpit/ambo, or place of the word, is also very important. (For detailed information about the altar and its appointments, see chapter 6.)

Seats in the chancel for worship leaders may be stalls, pews, or chairs. Traditionally, these seats were called *sedilia,* a Latin word for seats. For each worship leader, a prie-dieu may be provided to facilitate kneeling for prayer.

The chancel is furnished with various appointments and accoutrements that serve both practical and symbolic functions. Some are always used, while the use of others varies with the times of the liturgical year. The visual impact of worship appointments always needs to be considered in their placement, and visual pollution should always be avoided. It is vital never to obscure the central things—altar, pulpit, and font—with secondary and sometimes undesirable items (for example, overly abundant Christmas decorations or floral arrangements). Let the central things *be* central in people's eyes.

Furnishings

LINENS AND PARAMENTS   Altars have always been covered with fine cloths, known as linens, and paraments have adorned chancel furnishings since at least the fifth century. While linens are always white, paraments are in fabrics of various colors in order to reflect the liturgical day or season. White is a reminder of the purity and righteousness of the Christ who is unchanging, and it is an expression also of the light and joy Christ gives to his people. Our lives are constantly changing, alternating with joy and sorrow, birth and death—and with the hopeful time of Advent, the joyous days of Christmas, the revelatory time of Epiphany, the preparatory and penitential weeks of Lent, the incomparably celebratory time of Easter, and the weeks of growth after Pentecost. The colors of the paraments reflect these various times and moods, contrasting with the changeless light and love of our Lord. The basic characteristics of linens and paraments, and their functions, are the same across cultural lines, but the design and style of them may vary according to the cultural context of the congregation. (See later chapters for detailed information on linens and paraments and their care.)

CROSS/CRUCIFIX   A single large cross or crucifix is usu-ally placed near the altar for worship services, though its design and placement may take various forms. The most historic and traditional form in liturgical usage is the processional cross, which has been used since the fourth century; "fixed" altar crosses date only from the seven-teenth century and are not suited to flexible usage. Because the cross or crucifix symbolizes Christ's death and resurrection for our redemption, it should be promi-nent in size and of quality design and construction.

A processional cross is carried by its shaft in the entrance procession and placed in a floor standard or wall bracket in the chancel. It is also used for proces-sions outside the church (for example, on the Sunday of the Passion and the Day of Pentecost, or at graveside.) The processional cross may also be used for the gospel procession.

Processional crucifix

Otherwise, a fixed cross may be suspended from the ceiling above the altar or placed on the wall behind the altar. If the altar is not freestanding, the cross stands on the retable.

The most meaningful symbolic impact will occur if there is just one significant cross in a worship space, not multiple crosses. The multiplicity of crosses, ironically, diminishes rather than increases people's attention to this central symbol of our faith.

ALTAR CANDLES   Lighted candles are among the oldest ornaments of worship, as fire has long been seen as a sign of God's presence. In ancient times candles provided light for reading, but today they usually have only symbolic value (except, for example, for the Easter Vigil or Evening Prayer). In their most basic sense, candles are a visual reminder of Christ as the light of the world (John 8:12; 12:46).

At least two white candles are usually placed on the altar or in floor stands by the altar. If the altar is not freestanding, these candles are usually placed on the retable. With freestanding altars, especially, two candles or torches may be placed at one side, or one on each side. Or, four or six candles or torches may be divided between the two sides.

Candles for use in worship should be at least 51 percent beeswax so that they will burn evenly and slowly. Wider candles burn more slowly than thin ones. Candles need to be stored in a cool location. They become harder as they are stored, and thus older candles will burn longer. Electric or battery-powered "candles" are not authentic and should never be used in the chancel. Oil lamps are also not appropriate, and can be dangerous. Neither of these latter options burns down like a candle and thus does not mark the passage of time.

Candle with follower

Candle followers (sometimes known as caps) placed over the tops of candles will help prevent melted wax from dripping down the sides of the candles, promote even burning, and increase the life of the candles.

Clear glass followers are better than brass or other metal, as the glass does not detract visually from the candles and their flames. It is also helpful to use clear glass or plastic bobeches to line the base of the candle to protect the candle holder from wax. Both followers and bobeches are best cleaned in plain hot water while the wax is still warm (but put the wax in a trash container rather than the sink so it does not clog the drain pipes).

Candlelighters (also known as tapers) and extinguishers mounted on poles are used by acolytes and anyone else lighting candles. The wick in the lighter

Candlelighter/ extinguisher

needs to be kept trimmed, and the extinguishers need regular cleaning to avoid staining linens.

When small hand candles are to be held by the congregation for candlelight services, it is useful that the candles be inserted in the small cardboard or plastic candle drip protectors which are also known as bobeches. They prevent hot wax from dripping on and possibly burning the skin, and from dripping on carpet, pews or chairs, clothing, and so forth. The plastic bobeches (usually in white) are reusable and easy to clean. (See chapter 4 for information regarding care of candles and removal of candlewax stains.)

PROCESSIONAL TORCHES Torches are large candles placed in wooden or metal shafts that may be carried in procession just behind the processional cross. In design, the shafts usually match or coordinate with the processional cross. Processional torches symbolize the coming of Christ to lighten the darkness of the world. They are especially appropriate for festival days, as a way of giving visual emphasis to the festival being celebrated. Torches are placed in floor stands in the chancel, flanking the altar or sometimes the pulpit. Processional torches have been used to flank the gospel book for gospel processions since the time of the ancient church.

Paschal candle

PASCHAL CANDLE The paschal candle (sometimes called the Easter candle) is a large decorated candle that symbolizes our Lord's glorious Easter triumph over the darkness of death and sin. It is reminiscent of the pillar of cloud and fire that led the people of God to the promised land. Paschal candles have been used in worship since at least the fifth century.

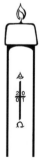

The paschal candle itself is at least thirty inches tall, and is placed in a floor stand, which is usually at least four feet tall. The paschal candle should be the largest candle in the space. Some great paschal candles in church history weighed three hundred pounds, and some stands were themselves ten feet tall—so important was it to symbolize the magnitude of Christ's Easter victory.

Paschal candle

As a part of the Easter Vigil liturgy on Easter Eve, the paschal candle is incised with a cross, the Greek letters *alpha* and *omega* (meaning the beginning and the ending), and the numerals of the current year. (Paschal candles are often sold with decals of these items. It is more authentic though to incise the actual inscription rather than rely on decals.)

The paschal candle remains in its central position in the chancel throughout the weeks of Easter, and it is lighted for all worship services during the season. On the Day of Pentecost, the paschal candle may be extinguished by an acolyte as the gospel reading concludes. After the final parish liturgy on the Day of Pentecost, the candle is moved to a place near the baptismal font and is lighted for each baptism and for funerals (but not at other times, as indicated below). It is a visual connection between baptism and Easter, reminding us that in our baptism we are buried and raised with Christ (Romans 6:3-5). Baptismal candles (see the chapter on baptism) are lighted from the paschal candle for presentation to the baptized.

A new paschal candle should be provided each year, for incising and lighting at the Easter Vigil.

For funerals, the paschal candle is carried immediately behind the processional cross, at the head of the entrance procession. It is placed in its stand at the head of the casket for the burial liturgy.

Evening Prayer candle

EVENING PRAYER CANDLE   The Service of Light (known as the *lucernarium*) in Evening Prayer begins with a procession in which a large, lighted candle (also thus known as the lucernarium candle) is carried into the darkened church and placed in its stand in front of the congregation. This candle should be almost as large as the paschal candle, but should be plain white, without decoration. The paschal candle itself is not used for evening prayer, because the symbolism and uses of the two candles are quite different. The paschal candle is a resurrection symbol, while the evening prayer candle is a more general reminder of the light of Christ.

GLOBE CANDELABRUM   Another type of "lamp" that developed in Scandinavia and has spread to North America is known as the globe candelabrum or light globe. The first one was designed for and placed in the (Lutheran) Cathedral of Uppsala, Sweden, in 1969, in connection with an ecumenical celebration; thus its increasing use in North America suggests both cross-cultural sharing and ecumenical/international prayer concerns.

Usually a globe candelabrum consists of a hand-sculpted world globe shape holding white (often votive) candles that worshipers light for various prayer intentions. Like many worship furnishings, globe candelabra are best designed for the given parish.

The light globe may be located in a variety of places, including the narthex, the rear entrance to the nave, at the side of the nave—the guiding principle should be that it is easily accessible to worshipers and to those who come to the church during the week to pray. In Uppsala, there is a calligraphic sign on the nearby wall that suggests lighting a candle while praying for someone who needs to see God's light in his or her life.

Globe candelabrum

SANCTUARY LAMP   Some churches have a sanctuary lamp in which a candle burns continuously throughout the year. The lamp is suspended from the ceiling or mounted on the chancel wall; it is never properly placed on the altar itself. In general, sanctuary lamps follow the ancient Jewish custom of always having a light burning at the altar and have come to symbolize God's living presence among us. As such, they are not extinguished following a service.

The altar itself, however, is a more powerful symbol of God's presence, and the sanctuary lamp is not regarded as essential in the worship life of Lutheran churches. In Roman Catholic and Episcopal churches, the sanctuary lamp near the tabernacle or aumbry signifies the reserved sacrament, and thus its use in the Lutheran context can be confusing ecumenically.

OFFERING VESSELS   Offering plates/baskets and an alms basin (or large basket) are used to receive the congregation's tithes and offerings at most services. These vessels provide a good opportunity

Ethnic offering and alms baskets

to make use of the people's own cultural traditions, such as baskets of traditional ethnic design. The offering plates/baskets are passed among worshipers, while the alms basin is customarily used by an acolyte or assisting minister in receiving the congregation's offering.

THURIBLE Also known as a censer, the thurible is a vessel that is typically suspended on chains, used for burning incense, especially in Evening Prayer during Psalm 141 ("Let my prayer rise before you as incense…"). The grains of incense are carried in a vessel known as an incense boat, and are sprinkled with a spoon onto lighted charcoal in the thurible. The rising smoke of the incense is a symbol of our prayers ascending to God (see Revelation 8), and its use in Christian worship can be traced back to the fourth century.

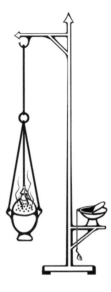

Thurible, incense boat and spoon

FLOWERS Since flowers are part of the beauty and frailty of creation, and are thus symbolic of our joy in Christ as well as earthly finitude, they are used almost universally to adorn the worship space. However, they are usually and appropriately omitted during the penitential times of the church year—Lent, most of Holy Week, and Advent. (See chapter 8 for flower suggestions for the liturgical year.)

Only the freshest flowers should be used, and their color and arrangement should be consistent with the season or festival being observed. Because flowers are used for their symbolism of life, joy, and human frailty ("All people are grass, and their constancy is like the flower of the field. The grass withers, the flower fades" [Isaiah 40:6-7]), artificial flowers have no purpose and no place in the worship space. Potted plants are not used on a regular basis in place of flowers, because they do not have the same symbolism of frailty and sacrifice as cut flowers.

During the growing season, flowers from parishioners' gardens and yards can be arranged for the worship space. Such natural offerings enable the space to be beautified without expense to the parish. They can be a genuine offering of a person or family in a way that a monetary donation to pay for florists' arrangements cannot be.

Flower vases usually coordinate with other worship appointments. Flowers in their vases may be placed in various locations, depending on the design of the worship space. They are not, however, placed on the mensa (the top surface of the altar itself), which is reserved for the eucharistic vessels, missal, and sometimes candles, nor are they ever to be placed in the baptismal font. Flowers and other decorations should adorn but never obscure the central things: font/pool, altar, and pulpit.

Central floral arrangements from Saturday weddings are customarily left for the parish to use the following day.

Flowers are usually distributed to the sick and the homebound at the conclusion of Sunday worship; they are not allowed to remain in the chancel until they wilt or wither. Vases are cleansed, thoroughly dried, and stored in the sacristy after each use; empty vases never remain in the chancel.

BANNERS Although they have been used since the sixth century, banners have only recently gained wide popularity. By their nature, banners are meant to be carried in procession and stored after each use, rather than to be placed as fixed or semi-permanent features in the worship space. The purpose of a banner is to employ colors and symbols to represent the day or season being celebrated. The best banners are visually symbolic and should not use words to convey their meaning.

Only well-designed and well-made banners, scaled to the size of their function and the space, should be used to adorn the place of worship. They should be used sparingly and never in a manner that clutters the space or obscures the central furnishings.

FLAGS National flags, being political symbols that mark the divisions of humankind, do not belong in a space where we celebrate our baptismal oneness as citizens under the sovereignty of God. Symbols used in the church should affirm the unity that all peoples can know through baptism into Christ; national flags are by their nature exclusive and thus are contrary to Galatians 3:27-28, which affirms our oneness in Christ. National flags, of course, may be placed in such rooms as fellowship halls (where they are often actually needed by scout troops and other groups meeting there).

The so-called Christian flag is unnecessary and superfluous in the space where we focus on the cross or crucifix.

SACRISTIES

VESTING SACRISTY   Sacristies are rooms, usually just off the chancel or nave, that are used for liturgical preparations and storage. Most congregations will want to provide two sacristies. One is the vesting sacristy, a private room in which vestments are kept and where the pastor(s) and sometimes other worship leaders vest and have prayer before the liturgy. (See chapter 3 regarding storage of vestments.)

This room should contain several copies of the congregation's worship book(s), including the *Occasional Services* book, a Bible, and a copy of the Revised Common Lectionary, a comprehensive church year calendar, pens and pencils, scissors, removable tape, and self-sticking memo pads for making temporary notes in service books, etc. The vesting sacristy should have a sink with antibacterial hand soap, paper towels, a full-length mirror, and trash basket. An attached restroom is useful. Other helpful supplies include a lint brush, safety and straight pins, nail clippers and files, comb, and facial tissue. If the parish uses cordless microphones, these are often best kept in the vesting sacristy. It is also very helpful to equip the vesting sacristy with a locked cupboard for safe storage of ministers' wallets, purses, and other valuables during worship.

WORKING SACRISTY   A second sacristy is the working sacristy, which functions as the headquarters of the altar guild or sacristans. Here are kept paraments, linens, sacramental vessels and supplies, candles and candle stands, flower vases, altar book and missal stand, a funeral pall and ossuary pall, hymn board numbers, oil for anointing, baptismal garments, thurible, incense and charcoal, and all other items needed for worship. The sacramental vessels and other items made of precious metal are usually kept in locked cabinets or a safe. The wine is also usually stored in a locked cabinet, or in a locked refrigerator.

In the working sacristy are also kept other needed items: iron, ironing board, antibacterial dishwashing soap, and clean towels or drying racks for cleansing eucharistic vessels, funnels for pouring wine, dustcloths and other cleaning supplies, stain removal supplies, metal polishes, a lint brush, first-aid kit, scissors, one or more knives, matches, sewing supplies, tools for flower arranging, cleaning supplies, paper and pen, and so forth. It is helpful if the sacristy has a bulletin board, a church year wall calendar which includes liturgical color designations (available from Augsburg Fortress; for sacristy purposes, a more comprehensive calendar including commemorations is published by the Ashby Co.), and a small reference library (see For Further Help, p. 130, for reference suggestions). The sacristy also needs hot and cold water, a sink with a regular drain, as well as a piscina—a sink with a special drain that goes directly into the ground for disposing of baptismal water (if water is not kept in the font) and wine remaining in the chalice (if it is not consumed by the ministers after the sacramental celebration). The working sacristy should also contain an easily accessible fire extinguisher that is kept charged.

In addition to storage, the working sacristy is also used for such tasks as cleaning sacramental vessels, polishing worship ornaments, arranging flowers, trimming candles, and mending paraments and vestments. Adequate counter space and storage in the sacristy are vital.

3. VESTMENTS

Then Moses said to the Israelites: See, the LORD has called by name Bezalel… He has filled him with divine spirit, with skill, intelligence, and knowledge in every kind of work done by an artisan or by a designer or by an embroiderer in blue, purple, and crimson yarns, and in fine linen, or by a weaver….
–(Exodus 35:30-31, 35)

As God's chosen ones, holy, and beloved, clothe yourselves with compassion, kindness, humility, meekness, and patience…Above all, clothe yourselves with love, which binds everything together in perfect harmony.
-(Colossians 3:12, 14)

Vestments are the distinctive garments worn by worship leaders (both lay and clergy) when performing liturgical functions. In various forms, vestments have been used since Old Testament times, although Christian vestments are derived largely from garments of the late Roman Empire. Vestments have both utilitarian and symbolic value.

There are several basic purposes for vestments. First, they designate particular liturgical functions. It has been almost universal in human history that people have worn particular clothes or uniforms for particular functions and particular occasions. For worship leaders, the vestments place less visual emphasis on the person and greater emphasis on the liturgical role being carried out, in order that attention may be given to God rather than to the *person* of the worship leader. Second, in their beauty, vestments reflect and witness to the beauty, majesty, and splendor of God. The beauty of vestments is primarily in their texture, form, and color, not in symbols sewn on them (a practice which is superfluous and thus discouraged). Third, vestments reflect the continuity of Christian worship through history. Worship leaders today wear essentially the same types of vestments that have been worn since earlier centuries of the Christian church. Thus, vestments provide a visual continuity with our ancestors in the faith.

Colors

Certain vestments—primarily stole and chasuble, but also dalmatic and tunicle, and often the cope—are to be worn in the color appointed for the day. The color assignments are also for most paraments. These appointed colors and their meanings are (see appendix A, p. 113, for their appointed days and seasons):

Black: ashes and mourning

Blue (royal): hope

Gold: triumph of the resurrection of Christ

Green: growth in Christ

Purple: penitence (in Lent); royal color of coming King (Advent)

Red: fire of the Spirit; blood of martyrdom

Scarlet: blood of Christ's passion and death

White: light, purity, and joy of Christ

In some cultures, the meanings of the colors are different. For example, in Chinese culture, white is the color of mourning and red is the color of celebration.

The Alb

The alb is a white ankle-length garment with close-fitting sleeves. It is the church's oldest and most basic vestment. Its name comes from the Latin word *albus*, which means white, and this whiteness symbolizes the purity, light, and eschatological glory of the resurrected Christ.

In the most basic sense, the alb derives from the white baptismal garment as a sign that the newly baptized has been clothed in the purity, righteousness, and eternal life of Christ. Thus the alb may be worn by both clergy and laity (assisting ministers, acolytes, choristers, and so on). Albs in colors other than white are not appropriate, for symbolic, historic, and ecumenical reasons.

As a vestment *per se* (beyond its basic baptismal reference), the alb derives from the white tunic worn by professional persons in the ancient

Alb

Roman Empire. Albs were worn by clergy for all services until the eleventh century, when the surplice (see below) began to be used for non-eucharistic worship. Today the alb is usually worn for all services except perhaps for the daily office (often known as daily prayer, which consists of Morning Prayer, Evening Prayer, and Prayer at the Close of the Day [Compline] in *Lutheran Book of Worship*), for which cassock and surplice have been traditionally worn.

The alb is gathered at the waist by a cincture (traditionally known as a girdle), a white rope or heavy white cord tied at the side or front. For clergy, the stole is placed through or tucked under the cincture. An amice, a rectangular neckcloth, has long been worn as a sort of collar with the alb. The amice originated as a means to protect the alb and other vestments from perspiration. Some contemporary albs have collars resembling amices.

When the Holy Communion is celebrated, the presiding minister usually wears a stole and chasuble (in the color of the day or season) over his or her alb.

CLERGY VESTMENTS

Stole

Ordained clergy wear stoles over the alb or surplice as a sign of their ordination into pastoral and priestly work. The stole is a symbol of the yoke of obedience to Christ. So closely connected are the stole and ordination, that the placing of the stole over the shoulders of the newly ordained is an integral part of the ordination rite, as the presiding minister says to the ordinand:

> Receive this stole as a sign of your work, and walk in obedience to the Lord Jesus, serving his people and remembering his promise: "Come to me, all who labor and are heavy laden, and I will give you rest. Take my yoke upon you, and learn from me; for I am gentle and lowly in heart, and you will find rest for your souls. For my yoke is easy, and my burden is light."
> –(*Occasional Services*, p. 197, quoting Matthew 11:28-30)

The stole, being the sign of ordination, is never worn by a lay person. (Hence, its use by choir members is unfortunate because of the confusion in meaning that results.)

The stole is a long, narrow band of heavy fabric worn around the neck. In historic usage, when worn with the alb for Holy Communion, the stole is crossed over the breast and tucked under or through the cincture. When worn for other services, the stole hangs straight in front, but is still tucked through or under the cincture. Stoles are not usually worn, even by clergy, for the daily prayer services (Morning Prayer, Evening Prayer, Compline).

It is not necessary to place symbols on stoles, for the stoles themselves (and their colors) are symbols.

Stoles, like chasubles, are worn in the appointed color for the day or season, and in fabric they often match the chasuble and sometimes also the altar paraments (or at least burse and veil). Multicolor or multi-season stoles are discouraged because they do not serve the important function of reflecting through color the meaning of the day or season.

In ethnic congregations, stoles (as well as chasubles and paraments) may be made out of a typical ethnic fabric (such as kente cloth in African-American congregations, or various kinds of silk or other Asian fabrics for Asian-American congregations). The color of the day should be respected, unless there is good ethnic tradition not to do so.

Alb and stole

Because stoles tend to slide and thus to hang unevenly, it is helpful to fasten them to the alb or cassock by means of a snap or hook-and-loop fabric fasteners at the back of the neck.

In some Christian traditions, deacons are ordained and wear a different type of stole. However, the practice of ordaining deacons is not done in most Lutheran contexts, and thus the deacon's stole is not worn. (Lay persons serving as *liturgical* deacons may wear dalmatics and tunicles for festive eucharistic liturgies, if the ordained pastor serving as presiding minister wears a chasuble. See later in this chapter.)

Chasuble

The chasuble is the principal vestment for the presiding minister during the celebration of the eucharist. It is a "full" vestment worn like a poncho over the alb and stole. (It is not worn over a cassock and/or surplice.) The fullness of the chasuble suggests that the eucharistic meal is intended to embrace all baptized people; thus, the chasuble is a reminder that the abundance of God's grace and the abundance of the eucharistic feast are intended for all of God's baptized family.

Chasubles are made of a wide variety of beautiful (although not necessarily expensive) fabrics. Their symbolism is in their fullness and color, rather than in any symbols attached to them. The chasuble has traditionally been decorated with an orphrey, a strip of contrasting fabric (most often gold) in the center of the front and back—either a straight vertical pillar or the shape of a *Y.* The orphrey does not include any symbols.

Chasubles are usually lined to enable graceful draping. Lightweight silk is often used. A contrasting color for the lining can be very beautiful.

It is ideal for the chasuble to match the stole, as well as to coordinate in hue with the paraments, burse, and chalice veil. The color is that appointed for the day.

Chasuble

OTHER VESTMENTS

Cassock

The cassock is not actually a vestment, but rather is a basic liturgical undergarment over which vestments are worn. Cassocks are black ankle-length garments, which are fitted from the waist up and have narrow sleeves. Cassocks usually button or snap all the way down the front.

Originally, cassocks developed as fur-lined garments used in winter in unheated European churches. They bear no symbolism.

For non-eucharistic services (especially Morning Prayer, Evening Prayer, and Compline), it has been customary for worship leaders to wear cassock and surplice. At eucharistic services the cassock may be worn under the alb if the additional warmth is needed. (Such use, obviously, is functional, not symbolic.)

Surplice
The full-sleeved white vestment worn over the cassock is the surplice. Surplices are at least knee-length, and they derive from the longer and more tailored alb. The whiteness of the surplice symbolizes the purity of Christ. The surplice is customarily worn over the cassock for Morning Prayer, Evening Prayer, and Prayer at the Close of the Day (Compline).

Cassock   *Surplice over Cassock*

Cope
The cope is essentially an ankle-length processional cloak or cape, often but not always ornate, adapted for liturgical use by clergy or lay liturgical ministers. It has been used liturgically since the ninth or tenth century. Copes are worn in the color of the day in the church year—although if a parish has only one cope, it should probably be white.

Copes are open in the front, fastened near the neck with a clasp known as a morse.

Copes may be worn over albs or surplices for festive services of Morning and Evening Prayer, and for ceremonial occasions such as the procession in a wedding, funeral, ordination, installation, or confirmation. A cope is also often worn by the cantor of the Easter Proclamation *(Exsultet)* in the Easter Vigil, and by the presiding minister for baptisms and for various orders of blessing and dedication. Copes are never worn over chasubles.

*Cope over alb,
with morse clasped*

Dalmatic

In congregations in which the presiding minister wears a chasuble for the eucharist, the principal assisting minister (liturgical deacon) may wear a dalmatic over the alb for festive celebrations. It is a less full vestment than the chasuble, but matches in color and fabric. (See illustration, p. 32.)

Tunicle

In congregations in which the presiding minister wears a chasuble for the eucharist and the principal assisting minister a dalmatic, the "junior" assisting minister (liturgical sub-deacon) may wear a tunicle for festive celebrations. The tunicle is even less full than the dalmatic, but the three eucharistic vestments match in fabric and color, although the orphreys or bands on the three are different (being simplest on the tunicle and most elaborate on the chasuble, with the dalmatic in between the two).

VESTMENTS FOR ACOLYTES AND MUSICIANS

Acolytes and musicians (especially choir members, also known as choristers) are also appropriately vested for their responsibility in worship leadership. Choirs, organists, cantors, and other musicians usually wear white albs, or black cassocks under white cottas or surplices. Robes resembling academic gowns are to be avoided, and persons who are not ordained do not wear stoles or pectoral crosses.

Dalmatic   *Tunicle*

For Confirmands

Confirmands sometimes wear white capes, or they may wear albs, both of which are a reminder of the white baptismal garment. Robes that are academic in style should be avoided, because they give an incorrect and inappropriate connotation to the confirmation rite—it is *not* a graduation, which is what the use of academic garments suggests.

For Bishops

Copes and Chasubles
Bishops often wear copes for liturgical functions, except when presiding at the eucharist, when they wear chasubles.

Pectoral Cross
A pectoral cross (from the Latin word *pectus,* which means breast) is a relatively large cross on a neck chain worn by a bishop. It is presented during the bishop's installation as an emblem of the office. In some cases, the judicatory has its own pectoral cross designed for use by its bishop during his or her term of office. Pastors who are not bishops do

not wear the pectoral cross; for them, the stole is the sign of ordination and thus of pastoral ministry. Lay ministers never wear either pectoral crosses or stoles.

Miter

Borrowing not only from ecumenical usage, but also from historic practice in a number of Lutheran church bodies around the world, some Lutheran bishops in North America have adopted the practice of wearing miters. These are stiff liturgical "hats" (double-pointed on top) worn with cope or chasuble when exercising episcopal function, including during some parts of some liturgical services.

Crosier

When in their own synod (and only then), bishops may carry a crosier (staff) as a sign of their office of shepherding.

SIZES OF VESTMENTS

While most clergy usually have their own albs, stoles, cassocks, and surplices, parishes should have albs and other vestments in a variety of sizes. This variety will serve not only pastors of various heights, but also lay assisting ministers and musicians. Stoles, chasubles, copes, and other vestments that fit a tall person will not be usable by a shorter person (perhaps a pastor supplying on a Sunday when the parish's own pastor is on vacation, an interim pastor, or perhaps the next pastor to serve the parish). Vestments should have a continuity of design and color.

CARING FOR VESTMENTS

The cleaning, storage, and preparation of vestments are usually the responsibility of the altar guild/sacristans. Vestments should be kept clean, fresh, out of direct sunlight, and ready to wear at any time, like any other good clothes for special occasions. Recognize that sometimes vestments must be ready for last-minute use, such as for a funeral. See chapter 4 for more detailed information on vestment care.

Most albs, surplices, and cottas are now made of washable fabrics, and may simply be laundered and pressed. Nonwashable fabrics and all other vestments require dry cleaning by professionals. Most vestments are stored on special hangers, but chasubles may be laid flat in large drawers in the sacristy; it is helpful to pad the folds with acid-free tissue or even towels to avoid creases and possible damage to the fabric.

It should be noted that while blended or synthetic fabrics (albs, for example) may be easier to clean and care for, they are consistently warmer to wear, and they may turn yellow when washed and dried.

For specific instructions on cleaning for and storing vestments, it is best to consult with their maker/manufacturer. Different fabrics require quite different modes of cleaning and storage.

4. BASICS

Who shall ascend the hill of the LORD?
    And who shall stand in his holy place?
Those who have clean hands and pure hearts,
    who do not lift up their souls to what is false,
    and do not swear deceitfully.
—(Psalm 24:3-4)

The altar guild is entrusted with the privilege of preparing the worship space for that gathering of God's family known as corporate worship. This ministry of preparation is as important to the worship life of the church as the pastor's preparation time or the choir's rehearsal. Meaningful worship does not simply happen. It requires prayerful and thorough preparation by all who are involved in it. The altar guild is concerned with the things of worship—the care of the worship space, and the care and placement of the furnishings, appointments, and ornaments used in worship. The overall goal of the altar guild is to see that the worship space is kept beautiful and in good order, both to glorify God and to provide a setting that helps enable the congregation to worship in a meaningful way. It is also the responsibility of the altar guild to keep the worship space ready for persons' individual use for prayer at times other than corporate services.

Sacristans and members of the altar guild are ministers of the liturgy, and they have several basic responsibilities. Housekeeping is one of the basic tasks, and it is best carried out with the attitude that it is a high privilege to care for the things that represent God's love and presence. The altar guild, along with the sexton, is responsible for keeping the chancel, altar, font, and pulpit clean and free of clutter. Linens, paraments, and vestments are cleaned regularly and kept pressed in readiness for use in worship. The sacramental vessels and other worship appointments are kept clean and polished. Adequate supplies of bread, wine, candles, and other necessities are secured and properly stored.

All work should be done with a full understanding of the meaning and significance of the items being handled. Members of the guild should know the names of the furnishings and accoutrements as a means of respect and reverence and to increase their efficiency. This learning, in turn, will help make worship itself more meaningful for guild members.

Routine Preparations

Certain routine preparations are done prior to any worship service (whether it is a Sunday morning eucharist, a funeral, a wedding, or another occasional service). Basic procedures (others will be determined locally) before services include at least the following:

1. Clean the chancel and see that all furnishings and appointments are dusted, polished, and in their proper places. Remove any items that will not be used.
2. Clean and press the needed linens and paraments, and put them in place. Be sure that the paraments are of the designated liturgical color for the day by consulting the church year calendar and appendix A, p. 113.
3. If it will be used, place the altar book on the missal stand and mark the propers according to directions from the presiding minister.
4. If there will be flowers, arrange them and put them in place.
5. Make sure that the candles are in place, with wicks upright and ready to be lighted. Check the candlelighter (taper) to be sure there is adequate wick and that the wick is trimmed, and clean the extinguisher of soot and wax if necessary. Provide matches for the acolytes.
6. Place correct numbers on hymn boards, if your parish uses them.
7. Put bulletins in place for ministers and acolytes.
8. Be sure that vestments for the presiding minister, assisting ministers, and acolytes are clean and pressed. (See chapter 3.)
9. For celebrations of Holy Communion or Holy Baptism, prepare the sacramental vessels, linens, and elements. (See chapters 5 and 6.)
10. If a processional cross and/or processional torches are to be used, be sure that they are ready for those who will carry them in procession, and that their stands are in place.
11. If there is to be an offering, prepare the offering plates/baskets and alms basin.

Other responsibilities of preparation for particular services and days are listed in the appropriate chapters.

After Worship

There are also routine procedures to be carried out after each service, in order to prepare the church as a place for prayer until the next liturgy. Sacramental vessels, flowers, flower vases, altar book, missal stand, processional cross, and torches are removed from the chancel. The flowers are prepared for distribution to sick and homebound persons. Among those preparing and distributing the flowers, the following or another suitable prayer from *Occasional Services* is appropriate:

> O Lord, look upon your servant, *name*. Touch *him/her* with your healing hand and let your life-giving power flow into every cell of *his/her* body and into the depths of *his/her* soul, restoring *him/her* to wholeness and strength for service in your kingdom; through Jesus Christ our Lord. Amen

The other items are cleaned and kept in the sacristy until the next liturgy. Empty vases and the missal stand are never left on the altar or in the chancel when not in use. Soiled linens and paraments are removed and cleaned. Any other items left in the chancel (such as bulletins, tissues, and worship books) are removed. Candle wicks are pulled into an upright position. Very important responsibilities following Holy Communion and Holy Baptism, including the disposal of remaining sacramental elements, are listed in chapters 5 and 6.

If the church building is open during the week for individual prayer and meditation, paraments should be changed according to the calendar.

Cleaning and Stain Removal

LINENS AND WASHABLE VESTMENTS   Linens for Holy Communion and Holy Baptism should be laundered and ironed after each use. The fair linen and credence linen should be laundered at least monthly and whenever they become soiled or spotted. Dusty, stained, or wrinkled linens have no place on the table of the Lord.

Laundering the linens and cleaning of vestments are responsibilities of altar guild members. The care of linens depends on the fabric content and its quality. In this chapter, the term *linens* refers to the items (fair linen, purificator, and so on), not to the type of fabric known as linen. Distinctions in cleaning and stain-removal instructions will be made between types of fabrics.

High-quality *linen* will provide long service when given proper care. Blended fabrics are easy to clean, and can be ironed damp. If washed in hot water, however, blended fabrics tend to "pill" with repeated washing. Follow the care instructions given by the garment manufacturer.

Ecclesiastical linens (whether made of 100% linen fibers or not) should not be sent to commercial cleaners. They should be laundered in separate loads in a washing machine's gentle cycle, or by hand. A mild unscented soap is used. Fabric softeners are not advised. Bleach, bleach substitutes, blueing, and starch *must be avoided,* since they are likely to damage any of the fabrics. Read the detergent labels carefully. Several rinses are helpful, and a small amount of white vinegar in the final rinse cycle will help remove soap and minerals in the water.

Blended-fabric "linens" and "wash-and-wear" albs, which are either polyester or made of blended fabrics, should be drip-dried after laundering, and then pressed while still quite damp. All linen or blended linen should not be machine-dried, as this breaks the natural fibers, thus shortening the life of the fabric.

The sooner stains are treated, the easier they are to remove. Lipstick stains on purificators and wine stains on various linens or on albs can usually be removed by carefully rubbing mild liquid detergent on the stain; repeating the procedure if necessary. For more stubborn wine stains, sprinkle with table salt, and pour boiling water through them until the stains disappear. Be aware, however, that many times red wine stains cannot be removed; this is one reason why white wine may be preferred for sacramental use.

Blood stains should be soaked in cold water and then laundered. Diluted ammonia will help remove dried blood stains from fabric.

Wax drippings on linens may be removed by scraping with a blunt instrument such as the back of a knife. Then place a white blotter, absorbent brown wrapping paper, or white paper towels under the linen, and press over the spot from the reverse side of the wax drippings with a moderately hot iron until the wax is absorbed by the paper. Remove the residual stain with alcohol or lemon juice, and then launder the linen. Another possibility for wax drippings on linens is commercial liquid wax remover, usually manufactured by candle companies. These removers must be used quite gently, however, and they work better for paraffin than for beeswax. Black wax spots can be prevented by keeping the candle extinguishers clean.

After laundering, linens should never be machine dried, nor should they be wrung, but rather rolled in towels to remove excess water; this works much better with linen fabric than with synthetic or blended fabrics (which should be drip-dried). Linen fabric items are most easily ironed while still quite damp, first on the wrong side and then the right side. It is important that they be perfectly dry before being rolled or folded for storage, or they will be uneven and rippled, and they could mildew. Folds are made by hand after pressing, not with the iron itself.

Fair linens, protector linens, and credence linens are stored rolled on heavy tubes and wrapped in acid-free tissue paper. Other linens may be laid flat in clean drawers or folded.

A very helpful and practical guide to the care of linens, including a detailed guide to stain removal, is available from: Masters of Linen/North America, 200 Lexington Avenue, Suite 225, New York, NY 10016. The manufacturer or supplier of your linens may also provide helpful instructions.

PARAMENTS   Paraments should be inspected weekly for soiling and ought always to be kept spotless. New stains are more easily removed than older stains. Paraments need to be cleaned less frequently than linens, but they require dry cleaning by experts. Instructions for such cleaning may come with the paraments and should be retained for reference. Even dry cleaning is a last resort, and it is crucial that the dry cleaners has experience in handling antique and other fine fabrics. In a city, try to find a dry cleaner that has done fabric cleaning for museum fabrics; try calling art museum curators for names of such businesses.

Be sure the dry cleaner understands that the dry cleaning must be done by hand, and that they must *never* press over embroidery, appliques, or metallic fabrics/surfaces on the paraments. For your protection, get a guarantee in writing. Candle wax can be removed from some paraments by the blotting paper and ironing method described above for linens. However, care is needed, and it may be best to consult an expert dry cleaner or the parament-maker.

Paraments may be stored flat in clean drawers, or by hanging over rods in special cabinets. Paraments should never be sharply folded, since this causes the fabric to warp and eventually to deteriorate.

CARPET   Wax drippings on carpets can be prevented most of the time by using followers (caps) and bobeches (drip protectors) on the candles.

(See chapter 2.) When drippings do occur, however, place blotting paper or plain brown paper bags on top of the wax, and press over it, repeating the procedure until the wax is absorbed. (The liquid wax remover referred to above, for use with linens, is not for use with carpets.)

Residual stains may be treatable with denatured alcohol or a dry-cleaning fluid—but be sure to test the substance first in an area that is not prominently visible. The best advice may be to contact the carpet manufacturer.

CANDLES AND CANDLEHOLDERS   In general, thicker candles burn more slowly, and therefore last longer than thinner candles. Solid beeswax burns the slowest.

Candles and candleholders require special care to prevent wax drippings. If candle followers (caps) and/or bobeches are used (see chapter 2) they must be removed and cleaned periodically. Remove them from the candles while the wax is still warm. Hardened wax can be removed from candle followers and candleholders (except those made of lacquered metals) by rinsing or soaking them in very hot water and wiping them with paper towels. Be careful, however, to avoid pouring the waxy water down the drain (where it will clog the drain). Scraping the hardened wax with a knife or fingernails is not recommended, since it may scratch the finish. For candleholders made of lacquered metals, soften the wax with hot air from a hair dryer, and wipe off with a paper towel.

Wax drippings down the sides of the candles themselves may be peeled off when the wax has become completely cold. The candles should be held in a clean cloth or with cotton gloves in order to prevent finger marks. Candles can be cleaned with some alcohol or vegetable oil on a soft cloth.

The soot and wax on candle extinguishers can be removed with very hot water and paper towels.

VESSELS AND OTHER FURNISHINGS   All of the vessels, furnishings, and ornaments used in worship should be handled reverently and cleaned carefully. In general, it is wise to wear soft cotton gloves when handling these items, since the moisture and oils of the skin will tarnish many metals and may mark candles. Whenever metal polishes are used, it is important to read and follow the instructions on the package labels. Sometimes it is advised to wear rubber gloves to protect the skin; however, it is also important with many vessels not to let the rubber actually touch the metal—so one hand might have a rubber glove on it, and the other a soft cotton glove.

Altar appointments and other worship ornaments are found in a variety of metals and other materials. The best policy is to obtain detailed instructions for their care and cleaning from the manufacturer. If this is not possible, certain general guidelines may be helpful.

Items made of brass may or may not be lacquered to prevent tarnishing. If they are lacquered, they should be wiped clean with a soft damp cloth and dried immediately with a clean soft cloth. Under no circumstances should lacquered brass ever be immersed in water, touched with detergents or abrasives, or polished; such procedures will damage the lacquer. When the lacquer begins to wear or peel, the item should be relacquered by a jeweler or the manufacturer.

Brass appointments that are not lacquered should be cleaned and polished frequently with a soft cloth and a fine grade of metal polish. Non-lacquered brass must never be touched with bare hands or damp cloths, since these cause tarnishing.

Silver and pewter appointments should be washed in hot soapy water, rinsed in clear cool water, and dried immediately with soft clean towels. Periodically (such as just before Easter, and one or two other times per year), silver and pewter items should be washed and then and polished with a good grade of silver/pewter polish. Never allow polish to dry on the surface. Since diamonds and other stones can scratch metallic finishes, it may be helpful to remove rings when performing these tasks.

When not in use, brass, pewter, or silver vessels and other appointments are best stored in clean cotton flannel bags to prevent tarnishing.

Porcelain, pottery, glass, and crystal vessels/appointments should be washed carefully with dishwashing soap (anti-bacterial soap for eucharistic vessels), dried thoroughly, and stored carefully. Do not clean them in a dishwasher. As with their metal counterparts, it is useful to wear cotton gloves when handling these items in order to prevent fingerprints.

Small individual communion glasses are often the most unhygienic mode of distribution of the blood of Christ. They must always be washed in hot water with anti-bacterial dishwashing soap, rinsed, allowed to air dry, and placed back in the trays with gloved hands. They should never be touched with un-gloved hands due to the problem of bacterial and viral transmission. This can be truly life-threatening to communicants who, because of cancer or autoimmune diseases, must take immunosuppressant drugs, and those whose immune systems are compromised by disease.

Each vessel and other item should have its place in the sacristy, with everything labeled to prevent unnecessary handling.

5. BAPTISM

Do you not know that all of us who have been baptized into Christ Jesus were baptized into his death? Therefore we have been buried with him by baptism into death, so that, just as Christ was raised from the dead by the glory of the Father, so we too might walk in newness of life.

For if we have been united with him in a death like his, we will certainly be united with him in a resurrection like his.

–(Romans 6:3-5)

The three central places of the worship space are planned intentionally and very directly for the three most central actions of corporate worship: the celebration of Holy Baptism—Christians are people "in the water" with our Lord; the proclamation of the word of God—baptized Christians are people who stand before the Book of Life; and the celebration of the Holy Communion—baptized Christians are people who gather at the table of the Lord.

Holy Baptism is our watery entrance into the church of Christ; it is the communal rite of Christian initiation into the family of God. Both historically and theologically there is a significant connection between baptism and Easter because baptism is a ritual but very real sharing of the death and resurrection of our Lord. As Saint Paul wrote (above), and as Luther expounded:

Baptism signifies that the whole [self] and the sinful birth of flesh are to be wholly drowned by the grace of God. We should therefore do justice to its meaning and make baptism a true and complete sign of the thing it signifies –(*The Holy and Blessed Sacrament of Baptism,* 1).

Baptism is our radically personal participation in the events of Good Friday and Easter, our threshold between death and life. It is the most important and most consequential event in our lives.

The way in which a parish celebrates Holy Baptism can emphasize the meaning and importance of this sacrament for a person's life—or, at worst, it can allow baptism to appear to be a merely perfunctory or sentimental act. A very important goal of every parish should be to accomplish Luther's goal—enabling the celebration of baptism in space (the font and area around it) and in action (how baptism is carried out) to be a "true and complete sign" of what St. Paul says it is: our sinful selves drowning with Christ and being raised to new life with him.

The altar guild's first responsibility in preparing for the celebration of Holy Baptism is to study the meaning of this sacrament. A clear understanding of the baptismal liturgy and an appreciation of the symbolic meaning of the items used (especially the water) will help baptism recover its central place in the Christian life (see For Further Help, p. 130, for reading and study suggestions).

During much of the history of the Christian church, baptism was celebrated only on Easter Eve, at the Easter Vigil. Such a practice underscores the central relationship between baptism and Easter. The Easter Vigil remains the ideal, most meaningful time for baptism, especially of youth and adults.

To restore Holy Baptism to its rightful place in the life of the church, many congregations are again celebrating baptism at the Easter Vigil, as well as on the Day of Pentecost, All Saints Day, and the Baptism of Our Lord (first Sunday after the Epiphany). Baptismal festivals on these occasions help keep baptism integrated into the unfolding story of salvation provided in the liturgical year. If your congregation observes such baptismal festivals, the altar guild may need to make preparations for the baptism of several persons. Occasions when several persons are baptized help preclude overly private understandings not only of baptism as a sacrament, but also of the Christian faith as a whole. Christianity is always personal, but it is never private.

Water and the Font
Water is the earthly element used for baptism. Water is an agent of both creation and destruction, both life and death, both birth and drowning. Throughout the Bible, water is a powerful image of God's saving acts. God created both land and water, and with water God continues to nourish and sustain all living things. The waters of the flood destroyed the wicked and saved Noah and his family. Israel was led through the sea out of slavery into the freedom of the promised land. Jesus was baptized in the waters of the Jordan River: later he used water to wash his disciples' feet, and he made water a sign of cleansing and rebirth, a sign of the kingdom of God (see the prayer of thanksgiving for baptism, *LBW*, p. 122).

In the waters of baptism, we are buried with our Lord. Our sinfulness, our otherwise ultimate destiny of eternal death, and the chaos of our lives are drowned in the waters of the font. We are raised up out of the water to share in the new life in Christ. Baptism is the most important event in our lives.

Water, of course, always needs to be held in a container. For Holy Baptism, that container is the baptismal font. The font is, at once, the tomb in which we are buried, the womb in which we are reborn, and the pool in which we are bathed.

Through much of church history, the size and shape of the font reflected the significance of baptism. Fonts in the late fourth to the sixth centuries, for example, were often pools as large as twenty-five feet in diameter, to accommodate the immersion of several persons. Often they were hexagonal or octagonal or cruciform (cross-shaped) (see below). Unfortunately, there has been a trend through the centuries to minimize the size of the font, with a resulting decrease in people's understanding of the significant meaning of baptism. Today many congregations are reversing that trend, realizing that the size and shape of the font help people recognize what baptism means for their lives. As *LBW* expresses it, "In Holy Baptism our gracious heavenly Father liberates us from sin and death by joining us to the death and resurrection of our Lord Jesus Christ."

Fonts are constructed of a variety of materials in several shapes. The most appropriate fonts are large enough at least to allow for the submersion (sometimes called total immersion) of infants, and some fonts

Cruciform baptismal pool

are adequate for the submersion of adults. Martin Luther strongly advocated baptism by submersion because that mode "speaks" the meaning of the sacrament. Cruciform fonts (shaped like a cross) probably best symbolize the meaning of the Holy Baptism.

The other two most traditional shapes are hexagonal (six-sided, referring to the sixth day of the week as the day of Jesus' crucifixion) and octagonal (eight-sided, referring to Sunday—traditionally known as the "Eighth Day" of the week—the day of Jesus' resurrection.) In our culture, the cross-shaped font is most readily understood, and it has practical advantages, as well.

Some fonts have covers, although they are no longer necessary. Font covers originated in medieval times when the consecrated water for baptism was believed to have magical powers. There were instances when people stole the water for magical purposes, so churches were required to keep the fonts covered and locked. Today it is unlikely in our culture that people will steal water from the font, and therefore font covers are superfluous. It is better to keep water in the font and to allow people to see and touch it and be reminded of their baptism. Depending on many local variables, water for a submersion pool may need to be filtered or mildly disinfected; it will always need to be heated when baptisms are scheduled. Questions of cleaning and filtration should be addressed to the pool's designer and/or builder.

The location of the baptismal font varies. There are, however, two guidelines. First, the location should suggest baptism as entrance into the family of God—and thus a location just inside the nave, perhaps in the center aisle, is meaningful. Second, the space around the font should be adequate for at least several persons to gather around it for the sacrament. There should also be space for the paschal candle, and it is helpful if there is a small table or shelf nearby for the ewer (if needed), baptismal garment, baptismal candle, towel, and oil. A credence table, covered by a small white linen, works well.

It is ideal and theologically appropriate for the font to have running water and a drain. If it is a small font that does not have these features, water is carried to the font in a large pitcher known as a ewer. The water should always be warm enough to be comfortable to the candidate. In a submersion pool, there needs to be provision for the water to be heated.

Other Items

OIL   Following the washing with water in baptism, the rite suggests that the sign of the cross be made with oil on the forehead of the baptized. This practice has been followed since the second century, but it derives from an Old Testament practice of putting a mark on the foreheads of persons whom God would save. The cross is a tangible reminder that in baptism we are united with the crucified Christ and sealed by the Holy Spirit. Olive oil is usually used for this purpose, both because it is easily absorbed by the skin, and because the olive tree is a traditional symbol of peace and reconciliation. The oil is known as chrism (from the same Greek word from which the title "Christ" is derived, referring to the "Anointed One"). The olive oil is usually mixed with a few drops of fragrant oil such as bergamot, because the fragrance is a sign of joy and gladness and also because it helps keep the oil from smelling rancid. Prepared chrism as well as fragrant oils that can be mixed with olive oil are available from ecclesiastical suppliers. Fragrant oil alone (not mixed with olive oil) should never be used because it is likely to irritate the skin.

Chrism is usually kept in a small glass or crystal cruet; the presiding minister then pours a small amount onto the inner lid of the cruet (if so designed) or into a small glass or crystal bowl at the time of the anointing. (An ideal vessel for this purpose is made by Meyer Vogelpohl—a six-inch-tall hand blown cruet with a lid that functions as an anointing vessel.) The cruet allows the congregation to see the richly colored oil. Some pastors still follow the older and more minimal practice of using a small oil stock for this purpose. The stock holds a piece of cotton, which is saturated with chrism. While this is convenient for taking oil to the sick for anointing, it is too minimal to use in a corporate liturgy for Holy Baptism. If it is used, however, the altar guild will want to change the cotton and pour in fresh fragrant oil every few months; heat (even room temperature) causes the oil to become rancid.

In some synods, or other regional gathering of congregations, oil is blessed at a service on or near Maundy Thursday. The oil may be received during a congregation's Maundy Thursday service, and then added to additional oil (if the oil received was just a tiny amount) for the parish's needs in the coming year.

Paschal Candle and Baptismal Candles

To emphasize the relationship between baptism and the death and resurrection of our Lord, it is traditional to place the paschal candle near the font (except during the weeks of Easter, when it is placed in a prominent location in the chancel) and to light it whenever there is a baptism or funeral.

In many congregations a smaller white candle is lighted from the paschal candle during the baptismal liturgy and presented to the newly baptized person (or parent or sponsor), to be lighted on each baptismal anniversary. Just as we honor physical birth by lighting candles on birthday cakes, baptismal candles can help us honor our spiritual rebirth in Holy Baptism. Lighting the baptismal candle from the paschal candle (rather than from altar candles) helps reinforce the important connection between baptism and Easter. It is usually the altar guild's duty to keep a supply of baptismal candles ready.

Baptismal Garment

A white baptismal garment may be presented to the newly baptized by a representative of the congregation. Known as a *chrisom,* the white garment is a visible reminder that in baptism we are clothed in the righteousness of Christ. The baptismal garment is also a symbol of the eternal life that begins in the font, a symbolism echoed by the white pall placed over a casket for the burial liturgy.

The garment may be quite simple, made by a member of the altar guild or someone else in the parish. For an infant, it may be a large rectangular white cloth with a center opening for the baby's head. For older persons, an alb is preferable, or a poncho-style white garment may be sewn. The baptismal garment should never resemble an academic gown or a bib.

Infant baptismal garment

In the African American tradition, several other presentations (salt, a band of kente cloth, a bracelet) may be made, reflecting additional images of baptism. As with the hand candle and baptismal garment, the presentations should not overshadow the central action of the sacrament: immersion in abundant water as our drowning and rising with Christ.

Preparations for Baptism

If water is not kept in the font at all times, it needs to be heated, placed in the ewer, and put near the font before the service in which the baptism is to occur. The font and ewer should be cleaned and polished prior to each baptism.

Other items also need to be provided near the font: a baptismal towel, white baptismal garment, and baptismal candle for each candidate. If a baptismal shell is used, it is laid on top of the towel. If anointing with oil is to occur, the oil cruet and any other vessels are placed near the font, and a purificator should also be provided for drying the presiding minister's hands.

After Baptism

After the celebration of baptism, if water is not kept in the font, it may be poured on the ground or into a piscina (a special drain in the sacristy which connects directly to the ground).

Adult Catechumenate

In the ancient church, it was primarily adults who were baptized, and this pattern lasted until about the eighth century in many places. Their baptisms were preceded by a two to three year period of formation in the faith known as the catechumenate—a period in which they were instructed in the teachings of the church; formed in how to pray, worship, and grow spiritually; and they learned how to serve people in need.

In recent decades, as many societies around the world have shown a decline in Christianity and many congregations in North America have realized the large number of people who were never baptized as infants, many churches have revised and reintroduced the adult catechumenate. The initial, tentative Lutheran rite for enrollment of candidates for baptism was in *Occasional Services* (1982). This rite does not require particular preparations by sacristans or altar guilds. A much fuller set of provisional adult catechumenal rites was prepared for Lutherans some years later under the title *Welcome to Christ* (1997) (see For Further Help, p. 130). Items to be placed in readiness by the altar guild or sacristans (in conjunction with the pastor) for the several rites are here noted:

For the Welcome of Inquirers to the Catechumenate, a Bible is presented to each catechumen (known as an inquirer to this point).

For the Enrollment of Candidates for Baptism, a large and beautiful book of enrollment (available from ecclesiastical supply houses—or it could be made within the parish, using ethnic art of the parish and the skills of a good calligrapher) is provided at a place in the midst of the assembly, where it can be seen and used easily. This is the book of names in which each catechumen signs his or her name. A pen should be placed by the book.

During the third Sunday in Lent, a "handing over" of the church's faith tradition occurs, and beautiful copies of the creed may be presented to each catechumen.

On the fifth Sunday in Lent the "handing over" continues by presenting the catechumens with the congregation's worship book, for it contains the core resources of the worshiping assembly: the creed, the rites for Holy Baptism and Holy Communion, the rites for Confession and Forgiveness, and Morning and Evening Prayer.

Preparations for the Easter Vigil, when the baptisms actually occur, are provided in chapter 8.

AFFIRMATION OF BAPTISM

When the rite of Affirmation of Baptism is used for confirmation, each confirmand kneels in front of the presiding minister in the center of the chancel. If there is no chancel rail, a prie-dieu is helpful. This is a prayer desk that assists a person in kneeling for the laying on of hands.

It is not necessary for confirmands to wear "robes," because they usually imply that the Affirmation of Baptism is a sort of graduation. If special dress is desired, however, simple white albs are preferred, because they are reminiscent of the white baptismal garment, thus providing a further visual linkage between baptism and its confirmation.

6. EUCHARIST

As they came near [Emmaus], he walked ahead as if he were going on. But they urged him strongly, saying, "Stay with us, because it is almost evening and the day is now nearly over." So he went in to stay with them. When he was at the table with them, he took bread, blessed and broke it, and gave it to them. Then their eyes were opened, and they recognized him.

–(Luke 24:28-31)

This account of Jesus on the road to Emmaus is an awesome witness to the power of God to reveal Jesus to us in the eucharist: the sacrament of bread blessed and broken, wine shed and poured—and all shared. Even when we do not perceive the presence of Christ in teachings or readings, we can experience his presence in his body and blood.

The word *eucharist* comes from a Greek word which means "giving thanks." Giving thanks is at the core of the church's main liturgy—the eucharist—the chief service of the church. It is known by many other names as well, including the Holy Communion, the sacrament of the altar, and the Lord's supper. By whatever name, this sacrament is the liturgy of word and table, the feast of the baptized family of God, gathered around the table of the Lord. In Holy Baptism we are initiated into God's family; in Holy Communion we are sustained in that family. In Holy Baptism we are made part of the priesthood of all believers; in Holy Communion we are nourished and strengthened to carry out our priesthood of witness and service in the world. In Holy Baptism we are joined to our Lord's death and resurrection; in Holy Communion we both proclaim his death and celebrate the feast of his victory. The eucharist is the birthright of the baptized.

This sacramental liturgy includes both proclaimed and visible Word—in it we hear the scriptures proclaimed in readings and sermon, and we see the Word made visible in the body and blood of Christ. Thus, the eucharist has two visual centers: the altar as the place of the meal, and the pulpit/ambo as the place of the word of God.

The altar guild has a special and privileged responsibility to prepare for this celebration that is so central to Christian worship. It is important for guild members to grow continually in the meaning of the eucharist and to be thoroughly familiar with the names and use of eucharistic vessels and linens.

Space and Furnishings for Word and Meal

Pulpit/Ambo

Pulpits, as we know them, have not always been used in Christian worship. In the earliest centuries of the church, when Christians met in homes for worship, preaching was usually done from the midst of the gathered people. In the fourth century, basilicas began to be built for worship. The altars were free-standing, and the bishop preached from his chair in the apse, behind the altar; other clergy preached from the altar steps or from an ambo (similar to a lectern). In the Middle Ages, as churches became larger, pulpits began to be used. Often the pulpit was placed part of the way into the nave, on the side, in order that the sermon could be heard by everyone. Pulpits grew very large and were often ornately carved or sculpted. Another development was having two places of the word—a higher pulpit or lectern for the reading of the gospel, and a less prominent lectern for the other readings.

Today there is an increasing tendency once again to have only one place of the word, rather than a separate pulpit and lectern. This practice visually reflects the connection between the biblical readings and the sermon. Whether it is known as a pulpit, ambo, or reading desk, it should reflect the dignity and importance of the word of God that is proclaimed from it.

The pulpit/ambo may have a parament known as an antependium, also called a pulpit frontal or fall. This parament should match the altar parament in color and fabric; the paraments are changed to reflect the day or season in the church year (see appendix A, p. 113).

One way to reflect the importance of the word of God is to flank the pulpit/ambo with tall candlesticks. The lighted candles symbolize the light of Christ that comes to us in the word. (It is especially appropriate to place the candlesticks by the pulpit or reading desk at non-eucharistic services, thus giving visual attention to the architectural center of the service.)

Lectionary

The readings should be read from a lectionary or Bible of a size and appearance that reflect the importance of the word of God. This book may be carried in the entrance procession and placed on the pulpit/ambo. To proclaim the readings from a small book or a flimsy leaflet is a poor witness to the significance of God's word.

Preparation for the Word

Prior to each service, the altar guild should be sure that the pulpit or reading desk is free of papers and books from previous services. The lectionary or Bible should be marked for the appointed readings, and placed in readiness for the entrance procession, or on the pulpit/reading desk (if the lectionary is not to be carried in the entrance procession). The proper parament is placed on the pulpit or reading desk. If desired, candles in tall stands are placed on the sides of the pulpit or reading desk, and the wicks are prepared for easy lighting.

Altar

The term altar is derived from the Latin word *alta,* which means high. The altar is usually on a raised platform known as a predella. Its height both enhances the dignity and the significance of the eucharistic table and enables the assembled congregation to see the actions at the altar.

The altar is the table for the Holy Communion meal—the place where the eucharistic feast is celebrated and around which God's baptized family gathers to share this feast. In the ancient church the altar was free-standing, and the presiding minister faced the people for the eucharistic celebration. During later centuries people were often considered unworthy to commune. The altar was moved against the east wall of the church, often far away from the congregation. The priest celebrated the eucharist with his back to the people.

The Reformation helped restore the Holy Communion to the people, and we are once again seeing altars placed in a free-standing position as tables, just as Luther and other early reformers advocated. In this position, the ministers stand behind the altar for the great thanksgiving in the Holy Communion liturgy, facing the people in a more courteous, hospitable, and intimate relationship. The free-standing altar witnesses to the meal character and fellowship of the eucharist.

The top of the altar is known as the mensa, which means table. The standard height of the mensa is thirty-nine inches, and it is usually rectangular or square. Five Greek crosses are often inscribed into the top of the mensa, one at each corner and one in the center. The crosses represent the five wounds of our crucified Lord.

The mensa is used only as the table for the eucharistic feast. Nothing is placed on it except altar linens, the missal stand, eucharistic vessels, and sometimes candles.

Altars which are not free-standing often have a retable, which is a small shelf above the back of the mensa. On the retable (which is sometimes also called a gradine) may be placed the altar cross, flower vases, and candles. Flower vases are not placed on the mensa itself.

Some older churches often also have a reredos, which is a high extension of the retable, made of carved wood or stone. When there is no reredos, an ornamental cloth known as a dossal is sometimes used as background for an altar that is not free-standing.

Altar Linens

Linens are traditionally used to vest the altar, marking it as the table of the Lord. They are on the altar at all times, except that they are removed at the conclusion of the Maundy Thursday liturgy, and the altar remains bare on Good Friday.

CERECLOTH The first linen traditionally placed on the mensa (the top of the altar) is the cerecloth. When the altar is stone, the cerecloth is waxed or otherwise waterproofed to prevent dampness from staining the other linens and from damaging the various vessels. With wooden altars, it is simply a heavy linen and helps protect the mensa, or the cerecloth may be omitted. When used, the cerecloth measures the exact dimensions of the top of the mensa.

When the cerecloth is removed from the altar, it is rolled carefully in order to prevent wrinkles, which in a waxed fabric will be impossible to remove.

PROTECTOR LINEN When a cerecloth is used, a second linen is placed over it, to which the altar parament(s) may be sewn. Known as the protector linen, it is the same depth as the mensa and the same width as the parament.

FAIR LINEN   The fair linen is the tablecloth for the feast of the Lord. The word fair refers to the fine quality and cleanliness of this linen. Thus, because of its function, and because it is very visible to the worshiping assembly, the fair linen should always be spotless, unwrinkled, and fresh. Each church will find it necessary to own at least two fair linens, so that one is always clean and ready to use. When laundered, the fair linen is never folded, but is rolled carefully.

The fair linen is the same depth as the top of the mensa, but its length may vary, depending on the altar and its paraments. Often the fair linen extends over the ends of the mensa one-third or two-thirds the height of the altar, or it may be the same length as the mensa. Generous hems (as much as two inches) help the fair linen hang straight and lie flat.

Traditionally, five Greek crosses are embroidered in white on the fair linen—one in the center, and one near each corner of the mensa. The five crosses symbolize the five wounds of Christ.

It is not appropriate to place lace edges on the fair linen.

Sacramental Linens

Four additional linens are used for the celebration of the eucharist: the corporal, the pall, purificators, and the veil. These linens are often carried to the altar in a burse.

CORPORAL   The corporal is a square of fine linen which is laid by an assisting minister on the center of the altar over the fair linen during the offertory (with the front edge close to where the presiding minister will stand). The eucharistic vessels are then set on the corporal. The corporal is one of the most ancient altar linens used for Christian worship.

Depending on the depth of the altar and the size of the eucharistic vessels, the corporal is usually about twenty inches square. A small Greek cross is sometimes embroidered in white near the center front edge.

The corporal is folded and ironed inside out in thirds each way (forming nine squares), so that it can be unfolded on the altar with the right side up. Thus, when it is refolded as the altar is cleared, crumbs of bread are folded into it and not dropped onto the mensa or the floor. The corporal may be carried to and from the altar in the burse (see below). A fresh corporal is used for each celebration of the eucharist, and each congregation needs several corporals. If there are multiple eucharistic liturgies on the same Sunday, a fresh corporal is used for each.

PALL   Used to cover the chalice before and after communion, in order to keep extraneous material out of the chalice, the pall is a linen-covered square of stiff cardboard, aluminum, or plastic. The size of the pall is determined by the diameter of the chalice, but it is usually about six inches square. The top of the pall is often embroidered in white with a cross or a symbol relating to the church year.

The linen covering the pall is usually sewn as a pocket, so that the stiff lining may be removed for laundering the linen. A clean pall should always be used.

PURIFICATORS   Purificators are square napkins, made of unstarched linen, used to wipe the rim of the chalice during the distribution. (Linen is preferred because it has the best absorption.) The size depends on the size of the chalice, since a purificator is draped over the chalice before and after the celebration, but the size is usually twelve to fifteen inches square. It is folded like the corporal, except right side out.

At least several purificators are needed for each chalice for each eucharistic service, so that the chalices can be properly cleansed after each communicant. When not in use during the liturgy, the purificators may be kept in the burse. Purificators are thoroughly laundered and ironed after each service.

VEIL   Several kinds of veils may be used. The chalice veil matches the paraments and vestments in the color for the day; when this veil is used, the burse matches the veil in color and fabric.

When a whole loaf of bread is used for the eucharist, a white linen veil—perhaps a second corporal or a large purificator—is sometimes used to cover it prior to the offertory.

Some congregations use a large white linen veil as a post-communion cover for all the vessels and elements.

BURSE   Sacramental linens may be carried to and from the altar in the burse, which is an envelope-like case. The burse often matches the chalice veil and paraments in the liturgical color for the day. It is constructed with two squares of sturdy plastic or cardboard, about nine inches square, each covered with linen and bound together on one side. The burse is also covered with another piece of fabric matching the paraments, and with a book-style hinge or pleated like bellows.

Congregations using chalice veils and burses will need a set in each liturgical color of the church year to complement the paraments.

Altar Paraments

Paraments adorn the altar in the appointed colors of the liturgical day or season, helping to make the altar the visual focus of the worship space. In pointing to the day or season through colors and symbols, paraments also serve devotional and educational functions. Paraments have been used since at least the fifth century A.D.

There are five different types of altar paraments in use: the full-frontal, the Laudian (four-sided) frontal, the superfrontal, the ante-pendium, and the frontlet. The type selected for a specific altar is influenced by the style of the altar, and may also vary according to the time of the church year.

A simple full-frontal covers the entire front of the altar, from the front top edge of the mensa down to the predella (floor). This type of frontal may be attached to the protector linen, which is then covered with the fair linen.

A Laudian frontal (sometimes known as a Jacobean frontal) covers the entire altar, hanging to the predella on all four sides of a freestanding altar or the sides and front of an east-wall altar. Laudian frontals are especially appropriate on festivals.

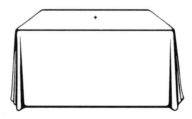

Laudian frontal

A superfrontal may be used alone or as a part of the frontal. It covers the length of the altar, but hangs down only ten to thirteen inches from the top of the mensa. Superfrontals are frequently used only with east-wall altars.

An antependium, narrower than a frontal, covers one-third to one-half the front of the altar. It may hang all the way to the floor, but usually is made to extend over the front of the altar about three-fourths the height of the altar. It is hung in the center of the altar.

Frontlets are hung down the front of the altar in pairs, usually only with eastwall altars. They are usually fifteen to twenty-four inches wide and fall about two-thirds of the distance to the predella.

Colors of Paraments

Congregations will find it useful to provide at least eight sets of paraments and certain vestments to accommodate the colors of the church year. The color of the paraments is far more important than any symbols placed on them. Symbols are not necessary or even desirable in most worship spaces.

White is the color of light, gladness, purity, and joy in Christ. White is thus the liturgical color appointed for festivals of Christ—the Annunciation, the Visitation, Christmas and its season, the Name of Jesus, the Epiphany, the Baptism of Our Lord, the Presentation, the Transfiguration, the fifty days of Easter (although gold is the preferred color uniquely for Easter Day itself), and Christ the King. White is also used for certain other festivals (such as the Holy Trinity) and commemorations, and it is the alternate color for Maundy Thursday. If seasonal symbols appear on paraments, it is wise to have more than one white set, (for example, one for the Christmas cycle and one for the Easter cycle) in order to relate each more closely to the varying times of the church year with their different visual symbols. The numerous occasions on which white and some other colors are used may also mitigate against their having any symbols at all. Without seasonal ornamentation, a single white set can be appropriately used for all white festivals, without being exclusively tied to any given time.

Bright red is the color of fire—the fire of the Holy Spirit. Red is used for the Day of Pentecost, for martyrs' days, and for certain other days celebrating events in the church, such as Reformation, ordination, and church dedications and anniversaries.

Scarlet is a hue deeper than red; it is the color of the crucifixion. Scarlet is used during Holy Week—from the Sunday of the Passion (Palm Sunday) through Maundy Thursday. The color should be selected carefully so that it is not confused with the bright red used for festivals.

Purple is the penitential color of Lent. It is also the alternate color for Advent, when it is interpreted as the royal color of the coming King. In congregations where paraments have symbols, and purple is used for both Lent and Advent, it will be helpful to have two different sets, with appropriate and distinctive designs on each.

Blue is the preferred color for Advent, because it is the color of hope, a central theme of Advent. Pale and navy blues should be avoided in favor of royal blue.

Green is the color of growth, and it is used during the seasons after Epiphany and Pentecost, to represent our growth in the Christian way of life and thought.

Gold is the preferred color for Easter Day, since that day is the "queen of feasts," the most important day in the church year. The use of metallic gold (not yellow) paraments on that one day helps to distinguish it in a special visual way from the remainder of the year.

Black, the color of ashes and humiliation and mourning, is appointed for Ash Wednesday. No symbols should appear on this bleak day.

Missal Stand and Altar Book

The missal stand holds the large service book for the presiding minister. It may be a wood or metal book stand, or simply a small cushion on which the service book rests for the celebration of the eucharist. The missal stand and altar book should be removed when not in use.

Eucharistic Vessels

Vessels used for the celebration of the Holy Communion usually constitute a matched set of fine metal such as silver or gold. Pewter, earthenware, or glass vessels may also be used. The appearance and material of the vessels should be worthy of the precious elements they hold—containers appropriate for the body and blood of our Lord. A minimum set of eucharistic vessels includes a chalice, paten, and flagon or cruet. If hosts (rather than a whole loaf of bread) are used, a ciborium or host box is also needed.

The chalice is the large cup used for the consecration and distribution of the sacramental wine. The cup portion of the chalice is attached to the base (or foot) by the stem. If the distribution is not by common cup, the chalice needs a pouring lip. In this situation, the wine is poured from the chalice into a small glass held by the communicant. (A drop of oil—olive oil will be convenient since there is probably already a supply of it in

Chalice

the sacristy—placed on the edge of the pouring lip will help keep the wine from dripping.) Individual glasses that are prefilled should not be used. Increasingly, congregations are making available the traditional common cup, because it is a fuller symbol of the unity we share in Christ.

Concerns have sometimes been raised about the hygiene of the common cup. Medical studies show, however, that the small individual glasses are far more likely to convey bacteria and viruses than the chalice because they are rarely washed in hot water with antibacterial soap, and they are usually handled at the rims with bare hands by altar guild members. If small cups are used, they should be sterilized between uses, and always handled with sterile gloves, never with bare hands. Disposable glasses are inappropriate to what they hold, and are probably no more hygienic than any other mode.

The paten is the plate used for the sacramental bread. Its size depends on the type of bread used. It is traditional practice for the paten to be set on the rim of the chalice for vesting in veil and burse. When a whole loaf of bread is used, however, another larger paten or basket is usually also needed.

Paten and basket

A flagon or cruet is usually used to hold the wine before it is poured into the chalice. The flagon is a tall covered pitcher, usually made of fine metal. The cruet is a glass vessel with a stopper, often topped with a cross.

When hosts (wafers) rather than a loaf of bread are used, they are kept in a ciborium or host box. A ciborium is similar to a chalice, but has a fitted lid. A host box (also known as a pyx) is a short round container with a lid.

Flagon and glass cruet

In some congregations the presiding minister ritually cleanses his or her hands prior to the great thanksgiving. A small dish known as a lavabo bowl is used for this. The water is poured by an assisting minister or acolyte over the presiding minister's hands from a cruet, and the hands are dried with a lavabo towel. This is a small linen towel, usually twelve by eighteen inches. It is folded lengthwise, right side out, in thirds, so that it will hang evenly over the arm of the assisting minister or acolyte.

A spoon is useful for removing foreign particles from the wine in a chalice. The bowl of the spoon made for this purpose is finely perforated.

SACRAMENTAL ELEMENTS

At the Last supper, our Lord took bread and wine, gave thanks to God, and declared that

Host box and ciborium

they were his body and blood. He shared the bread and wine with his disciples, and told them to "Do this for the remembrance" of him. After his crucifixion and resurrection, he revealed himself to two of his disciples on the Emmaus road in the breaking of bread. Christ's followers of all times have had an insatiable appetite for this bread and wine, because they know that in them the Lord himself is present. When the prayer and actions of the upper room are repeated by the presiding minister, we share the very life of the crucified and risen Christ. The Lord is truly present "in, with, and under" the bread and the wine in the Holy Communion.

Bread signifies several things biblically and in our own time. The ancient Israelites believed that bread came from the hands of God—and indeed, it does. Bread also carried the image of death and resurrection: the wheat seed is buried in the earth, where it comes to life and sprouts; and then the grain is crushed to be harvested so that flour can be made and bread can rise. Bread also, of course, satisfies basic human hunger.

The early Christian church always used ordinary bread for Holy Communion, a practice that is still preferred. A whole loaf of bread has advantages over individual wafers, because the one loaf is a powerful symbol of our unity in Christ: "When we break the bread, is it not a means of sharing in the body of Christ? Because there is one loaf, we, many as we are, are one body; for it is one loaf of which we all partake" (1 Corinthians 10:16-17, NEB). The breaking and sharing of the bread is a symbol also of our Lord's crucifixion, a witness to his own body being broken on the tree of the cross.

Carefully made homemade wheat bread is particularly good for the eucharist, for it is a visual reminder that God takes common earthly elements and human labor and uses them for extraordinary purposes. Bread that crumbles easily should be avoided. Several sacramental bread recipes are provided later in this chapter.

When a whole loaf of bread is used, provision should be made for cleaning the chancel after the service.

Wine is used for the Holy Communion because that is what Christ used in the upper room and directed us to use when we celebrate his holy meal. In addition, wine is used because of its unique meaning. While Psalm 104 speaks of bread for strength, it speaks of wine for gladdening our hearts. Bread was a staple in ancient Jewish meals, but wine was used only for festive occasions. The purpose of wine was not to quench thirst, but to give joy and life. Thus, wine is not only the blood of Christ through its use by him; it is also a sign of the festive and joyful nature of the eucharistic meal.

The wine may be homemade, purchased commercially, or purchased from an ecclesiastical supplier. A fine dinner wine should be used, avoiding sweet port. Only wine made from grapes should be used. The wine may be white or red. Red, however, is more difficult to remove from linens. (Regarding wine stain removal, see chapter 4.)

CREDENCE AND OFFERTORY TABLE

The credence is a small shelf or table near the altar on which the eucharistic vessels and missal stand are kept prior to the offering. Many churches have two credences—one for the sacramental vessels and one for the offering plates and alms basins.

The offertory table is a small table near the rear of the nave where the bread and wine are placed until they are carried forward along with the monetary offering, during the offertory. Both the credence and offertory tables are covered with white linen cloths.

SETTING THE TABLE OF THE LORD

Preparation of the altar for the eucharistic feast should be done well ahead of the celebration. Before the first actual tasks comes prayer and the attitude of reverence. Most important in all of the preparatory work is that it be done with the reverence and good order that befit Christ's presence. Awareness of Christ's presence in the sacrament will ensure that the work is done with genuine joy and gratitude for God's grace. To prepare the Lord's table is an immense privilege. The following prayers from *Lutheran Book of Worship,* or similar prayers, may be helpful in the sacristy before beginning your work:

> Bless us, O God, with a reverent sense of your presence, that we may be at peace and may worship you with all our mind and spirit; through Jesus Christ our Lord. Amen

> O Jesus, our great high priest, be present with us as you were present with your disciples and make yourself known to us in the breaking of bread. Amen

The first actual tasks, after prayerful preparation, are to be certain that the chancel and its furnishings are clean, that unnecessary items are removed, that the correct paraments are in place, that all linens are freshly laundered and ironed, that all of the sacramental vessels are clean and polished, and that sufficient quantities of bread and wine are ready.

There are various acceptable ways of arranging the vessels for the eucharist. The method used in a given parish will be determined by the available chancel furnishings and vessels, by the pastor's preferences, and by a sense of good liturgical order.

In determining parish customs, the altar guild and the pastor must first ascertain the resources of the church. Is the credence to be used? Is the altar free-standing? Are burse and veil to be used? Is the paten a proper size to fit into the rim of the chalice? Is there an offertory procession? Is the pastor right- or left-handed? Are there lay assisting ministers? Answers to questions such as these will help in selecting a method for preparing the table of the Lord.

The chalice is often vested in the traditional manner prior to the liturgy. Vesting requires several steps:

1. A purificator folded in thirds lengthwise is placed over the mouth of the empty chalice, so that the right and left sides hang evenly over the edges of the chalice.

2. The paten is placed on top of the purificator. (If hosts rather than a whole loaf are to be used, a large host may be placed on the paten.)

3. The paten is covered with the pall.

4. The chalice veil in the proper color of the day is placed over the pall and arranged so that a trapezoid is seen when viewed from the front.

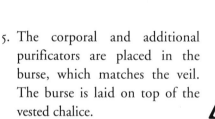

5. The corporal and additional purificators are placed in the burse, which matches the veil. The burse is laid on top of the vested chalice.

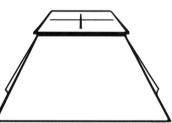

It is preferable for the vested chalice (as well as flagon and other vessels) to be kept on a credence until the offering, at which time an assisting minister carries it to the altar and sets the table. However, if there is no credence, the vested chalice may be set on the altar prior to the service. It is carried by holding the stem of the chalice with one hand, with the other hand flat on top of the burse to steady it.

During the offering, the corporal is placed on the altar, and the vessels are set on the corporal. Sometimes this placement is the task of an altar guild member or sacristan. Note that it does not matter whether the missal stand is to the presider's right or left—it is best to ask the presider for his/her preference. If the missal is placed to the right of the corporal, then the burse is placed to the left. If a large white veil is used rather than a burse, the veil is folded and placed to the side of the corporal in place of where the burse is shown in these diagrams.

The following arrangement is appropriate when a whole loaf of bread is used:

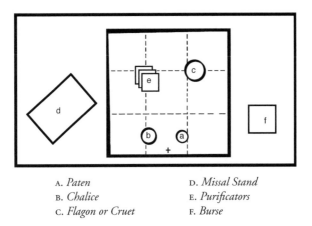

A. *Paten*   D. *Missal Stand*
B. *Chalice*   E. *Purificators*
C. *Flagon or Cruet*   F. *Burse*

If hosts are used, the following arrangement may be employed:

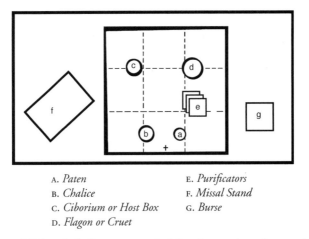

A. *Paten*   E. *Purificators*
B. *Chalice*   F. *Missal Stand*
C. *Ciborium or Host Box*   G. *Burse*
D. *Flagon or Cruet*

When additional chalices are needed for the service, they are brought to the altar and filled just before the distribution; only one chalice is on the altar for the great thanksgiving.

OTHER PREPARATIONS

Depending on local practices, the altar guild may have additional responsibilities in preparing for the Holy Communion.

In some congregations, communion registration cards are placed in pew racks in order that a record can be kept of communicants. It is also important to be sure that sharpened pencils are in place.

In congregations where the common cup is not used exclusively, it is necessary for trays of individual glasses to be set out for distribution as communicants approach the altar. These glasses should never be pre-filled, because that practice further weakens the symbolism of our oneness in Christ and suggests an overly individualistic understanding of the sacrament.

When the elements are to be carried to the sick and homebound following the congregation's service (using the rite of Distribution of Communion to Those in Special Circumstances, *Occasional Services,* pp. 76–81), adequate bread and wine must be provided prior to the service so they can be consecrated during the Great Thanksgiving. In addition, the vessels for carrying the elements and the purificators need to be prepared (see the end of this chapter).

FOLLOWING THE SERVICE

After the liturgy is concluded, all of the eucharistic vessels and linens are removed from the chancel and taken to the sacristy for cleaning. Unused hosts are stored in a cool and dry place for future use, keeping separate those which have been consecrated. The remains of a loaf of bread should be eaten by the ministers and the altar guild, and shared with others if a large amount remains. Wine remaining in the chalice may be consumed by the ministers and others, or poured into a piscina (a special drain going directly into the ground) or directly into the ground.

Vessels are thoroughly washed in hot soapy water and dried with soft cloths. Once cleaned, they should be handled with soft, dry gloves or cloths in order to prevent marking them. If polishing is needed, see the instructions in chapter 4 or as provided by the manufacturer.

All sacramental linens should be laundered and ironed after each use. Instructions for cleaning and stain removal are provided in chapter 4.

EUCHARISTIC BREAD RECIPES

Communion Bread
This simple recipe is courtesy of Cynthia Fazzini, and is included in John Dornheim's sacramental bread recipe collection, *And He Took a Loaf of Bread.*
5 ½ cups bread flour
2 cups water
1 package yeast
1 teaspoon salt

Dissolve yeast in warm water. Sift in flour. Knead for 10 minutes. Let rise for 1 ½ to 2 hours. Punch down. Knead again, for about 2 minutes. Shape into four round loaves. Score top, or use a eucharistic bread stamp. Bake at 350° for 20–25 minutes.

Pita
Pita is a flat, round, hollow bread (sometimes referred to as "pocket bread") which is eaten extensively in biblical lands. It is good for sacramental use because of its size, shape, and ease in handling. The following recipe is from Israel, courtesy of Avraham Har.

Dissolve 2 packages of yeast in 1 cup of lukewarm water.
Add 1 teaspoon of salt and 2 ½ cups of white flour to the water, and stir.
Knead lightly, and let the dough rise in a warm place for approximately 1 hour.
Knead the dough again.
Divide the dough into 8 equal parts.
Form each part into a ball, and place on floured waxed paper.
Let the balls rise again for about 30 minutes.
Preheat the oven to 500° for at least 15 minutes.
Roll each ball on floured paper into a circle about 4 inches in diameter.
Flour 2 cookie sheets.
Arrange 4 balls on each sheet.
Place the cookie sheets in the middle of the oven, and bake for about 3 minutes.
The bread will look puffed in the middle, and the outside will be off-white with brown spots.

After cooling, the pita bread should be wrapped tightly to prevent drying. It may be stored in a refrigerator for several days. For longer storage, wrap well and freeze.

Flat Whole Wheat Bread

This recipe makes 4 flat 10-inch loaves, each of which will serve about 200 communicants. It is provided by Pat Frost, of St. Paul Lutheran Church, New City, New York.

Preheat oven to 375°.
Mix together the following ingredients:
6 ½ cups whole wheat flour
¼ cup olive oil
2 tablespoons honey
1 teaspoon salt
2 ½ cups warm milk
2 eggs

Divide the dough into 4 sections. Knead each section on a floured breadboard, and roll out each to make a 10-inch circle.
Slightly oil cookie sheets with a paper towel. On cookie sheet, carefully score each loaf vertically and horizontally, with spaces about ⅛ inch wide; do not score through to bottom.
Bake for 20 minutes.
Put on racks to cool.
These loaves may be frozen for storage. The recipe may be halved.

Whole Wheat Communion Bread

This recipe is courtesy of Jay Rochelle, and takes less than 45 minutes from start to finish.
1 ½ cups whole wheat flour
½ cup white flour
¼ teaspoon salt
¾ teaspoons baking soda
2 heaping teaspoons oil
¾ cup cold water
3 tablespoons molasses or honey or a mixture

Mix dry ingredients. Add oil and blend well. Add water and honey/molasses and mix. Knead about 2 minutes. Roll out to ¼ inch thick. Cut into 6-7 inch rounds (making 3-4 flat loaves). Bake about 15 minutes at 350° on an ungreased cookie sheet.

See the For Further Help section, p. 130, for information on a large collection of sacramental bread recipes compiled by John Dornheim.

COMMUNION OF THE SICK AND SHUT-IN

Occasional Services provides two rites for communing "those in special circumstances," by which is meant those baptized who are sick, hospitalized, or homebound for an acute, chronic, or terminal illness, or for reasons of disability which preclude leaving one's home. The traditional home communion rite to be celebrated by pastors is provided with the title "Celebration of Holy Communion with Those in Special Circumstances." Another rite, for leadership primarily by laity, is provided with the title "Distribution of Communion to Those in Special Circumstances." In the first, the pastor celebrates an abbreviated form of the "usual" eucharistic liturgy. In the second, a lay minister trained for the purpose distributes bread and wine remaining from that morning's eucharistic liturgy to those who were unable to attend by reason of sickness or physical disability; this distribution is to follow the congregation's liturgy immediately.

Vessels for these rites need not be expensive, but they should be appropriate to their purpose. Small glass cruets with leakproof stoppers are appropriate for the wine. A small chalice designed for home communions may be used, or a simple wine goblet from a home may be used. Disposable "communion glasses" are not appropriate for sharing the blood of Christ. Metal, glass, or ceramic boxes made for the purpose are appropriate for the bread. A pewter set of vessels in a simple pouch, made especially for the lay distribution rite, is made by Augsburg Fortress.

The amount of wine and bread should be carefully estimated so that there is a sufficient quantity, without a great amount remaining. Purificators should be provided in adequate quantity.

The elements for the distribution rite led by laity are taken from consecrated bread and wine remaining from the congregation's eucharist. The wine should be taken from that remaining in the flagon or other such vessel—not from a chalice from which congregants have received.

Each week the altar guild or sacristan should thoroughly wash all vessels used for these two rites with anti-bacterial soap, drying them with clean towels that have been bleached.

7. RITES

Then we your people, the flock of your pasture,
will give thanks to you forever;
from generation to generation we will recount your praise.
–(Psalm 79:13)

In addition to liturgies that are used regularly and frequently and are central to the life of the congregation, such as Holy Communion or Evening Prayer, there are various rites for specific occasions. These are known as "occasional services," and they are for use at particular times in the lives of individuals as well as in the corporate life of the church. Three of these rites (Affirmation of Baptism, Marriage, and Burial of the Dead) are provided in *Lutheran Book of Worship* and are covered in other chapters of this manual. Others of these rites are provided in the *LBW* companion volume, *Occasional Services*. A few African American rites are provided in *This Far by Faith,* and some Hispanic-background rites are included in *Libro de Liturgia y Cántico.*

HEALING RITES

Occasional Services provides two healing rites, one for use with the assembled congregation (or a specially gathered group), and one for use with individuals in their homes or hospitals, nursing homes, or other assisted living or rehabilitation facilities. The preparations for each of these types of healing rites are virtually the same, as are their meaning and purpose.

The Service of the Word for Healing is a corporate rite (for use with the assembled congregation or a group of persons gathered for this purpose) of readings, prayer, and the laying on of hands and anointing. It is not intended for use on Sunday mornings at the chief service of the congregation, though it may be used or be integrated into the eucharistic liturgy at other times when the focus can be specifically on healing, for example, a Sunday (or other) afternoon or evening. The liturgical color for such corporate rites is that appointed for the day or season in the year.

When this service is scheduled, the altar guild needs to prepare the oil for anointing and supply a purificator for wiping the minister's hands after the anointing. Both items may be placed on a credence before the service.

Oil has long been used in anointing the sick (see Mark 6:13 and James 5:14). In biblical times, oil was used as a medicine; the Good Samaritan put oil on the wounds of the traveler on the road to Jericho. Oil is also a symbol of peace and of the Holy Spirit. Olive oil is traditionally used for anointing, both because it is easily absorbed by the skin and because the olive branch is an ancient symbol of life and peace. (Other meanings of olive oil for anointing are provided in chapter 5.)

The oil for anointing may be placed in a small glass cruet with a lid into which the oil can be poured for the anointing. The older practice of using an oil stock containing cotton, which is moistened with the oil, minimizes the symbolic value as well as the olfactory impact of the oil, and is best limited (if a stock is used at all) for anointing in hospitals or other individual settings. (See the section on oil in chapter 5 for a specific suggestion regarding a vessel for the oil.)

It should be kept in mind that olive oil will become rancid in sunlight, and will oxidize in contact with air. It is best stored in a cool, dark place between anointings. Glass display cases are perhaps the worst way to keep the oil, for it will deteriorate rapidly. Discarded oil (and the cotton from a stock, if used) is burned.

Marriage

Weddings are public worship services focused on God, not private ceremonies focused on people. The congregation gathers to worship God who is the source of love, and, in that worship, to witness the marriage of a man and a woman. When this is kept in mind, many issues regarding the preparation for weddings are clarified.

Weddings are not appropriate during Holy Week, because of the solemn and penitential nature of that week.

Paraments for weddings are in the liturgical color for the day—for whatever day or season in the church year it happens to be. It is not appropriate to use white paraments, for example, if white is not the appointed color in the church year. The bride and groom should be informed about the liturgical color well in advance of the wedding, so that dresses and flowers may be selected to coordinate (or at least not clash) with it.

The altar guild oversees the decorating of the church for weddings, and is responsible for ensuring that the altar is not obstructed and that propriety is maintained. Flowers and other decorations should not interfere with movement in the liturgy, and all decorations and floral arrangements should be appropriate for corporate worship. Flowers are not placed directly on the mensa, or surface, of the altar.

Kneeling cushions or a prie-dieu are placed in the position indicated by the presiding minister. It is important that they be kept clean.

Candles near the altar are whatever would normally be there for worship. Additional candles and candelabra are optional, based on the wishes of the couple and subject to approval by the pastor. Usually the cost of any additional candles is borne by the couple.

The "unity candle" (a ceremony in which the bride and groom light a single candle and extinguish their two separate candles) is theologically inappropriate and should not be used in church weddings. Bride and groom do not "extinguish" their individual lives when they are married, and to use such a ceremony reflects a deficient understanding of marriage. In addition, such a ceremony tends to overshadow the central acts of the exchange of promises and the giving of rings.

The marriage service may be celebrated within the liturgy for Holy Communion if both the bride and groom are baptized and eligible to commune according to church polity. The eucharist is never received by the couple alone, however, because it is always a congregational celebration, open to all who are baptized. If the eucharist is celebrated, see chapter 6 regarding preparations for it.

After weddings, the altar guild is responsible for putting the chancel in order for the next worship service. If flowers are left by the wedding party, they should be used again only if they remain appropriately fresh. Otherwise, they may be taken to persons who are sick or homebound. Empty vases should, as always, be removed from the chancel.

BURIAL OF THE DEAD

Church funerals are corporate worship services, and everything about them should proclaim Christ's resurrection. Accordingly, the coffin is closed before the service begins and remains closed throughout the service.

Paraments and vestments are in the appointed color for the day or season of the church year.

Flowers may adorn the altar, and the color may be selected to coordinate with the paraments, appropriate to the time in the church year. Other flowers, especially large sprays with organizational or fraternal insignia, are not brought into the worship space since they tend to direct attention away from the altar. Some of these arrangements may be placed in other parts of the church, such as the narthex, or gathering and reception areas, and then taken directly to the cemetery.

Every congregation should provide a white funeral pall, which is used to cover the coffin while it is in the nave. The pall is a reminder that in Holy Baptism we have been clothed in the righteousness of Christ and that eternal life began in baptism. The white pall thus echoes the white baptismal garment, which the fourth-century theologian John Chrysostom called the "garment of immortality." In addition, the pall enables all coffins to come equally before the altar, a reminder that God loves everyone, rich and poor alike. The pall may be laid over the last pew in readiness for the burial liturgy. It is placed over the coffin at the beginning of the burial liturgy, before it is carried into the nave. The pall may be removed from the coffin at the church door after the service in the church. It is possible for members of the altar guild, or other members of the parish, to make a white pall in a quilted style.

Flowers are never placed on top of the pall. The altar guild should ensure that the pall is clean and wrinkle-free for each funeral in the church.

Prior to the service, the altar guild places the paschal candle stand near the head of the center aisle. If processional torches are used instead, their stands are placed near where the head and foot of the coffin will be. The processional cross stand is put in its usual place in the chancel.

The coffin is carried in procession from the narthex to the front of the nave for the burial liturgy, and the altar guild/sacristans may be asked to help form the procession in the narthex. The order for the procession is: processional cross, paschal candle and/or torches, presiding minister, assisting minister(s), pallbearers and coffin, and the bereaved. The coffin is then placed at the front of the nave in the center aisle at a right angle to the altar. The head of the coffin is nearest the congregation (unless the deceased person was ordained, in which case the head is placed closest to the altar).

Increasingly, the burial rite is placed within the liturgy for Holy Communion. This practice both proclaims Christ's victory over death, and gives strength to cope with grief. See chapter 6 regarding preparations for the eucharistic liturgy. The eucharist is available to all baptized persons who are present.

Following the service, the pall is removed (carefully, to prevent soiling it) from the coffin at the door of the church and is stored carefully. The processional cross and torches are stored in the sacristy or elsewhere for future use (the processional cross may accompany the coffin to the place of burial). The paschal candle is returned to its proper place—near the altar during the weeks of Easter, and near the baptismal font during the remainder of the church year. Empty flower vases are always removed from the chancel. Flowers not taken to the grave may be shared with the sick and homebound.

Increasingly, persons are choosing cremation, often with burial in a columbarium. Likewise, many parish churches are now constructing various types of columbaria. A columbarium may consist of a brick or stone wall, inside the church or out of doors on the church grounds, with individual niches for small urns of ashes, with plaques naming the individual. Alternatively, it may be constructed more simply as a garden in the church courtyard or elsewhere on the grounds close to the church building. In the latter case, the ashes themselves (without an urn or other container) are scattered over and mixed with the soil

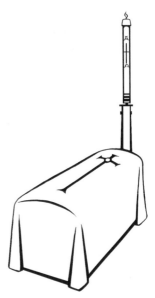

Coffin with white funeral pall and paschal candle

Ossuary urn with white linen pall and paschal candle

and thus with the ashes of others buried there. This type of columbarium is often called a memorial garden, and usually there is a larger plaque or tablet naming those whose ashes are interred there.

When cremation is employed, a small white pall may be used to cover the urn containing ashes (known as an ossuary) for the memorial service (much as the larger funeral pall is used for coffins). The ossuary may be set on a small table near the front of the nave, along with the paschal candle; the urn would be in the same location as the coffin in the funeral liturgy.

ORDINATION

Ordinations are often celebrated at a synodical service, with the bishop ordaining several persons at once. Ordinations may also take place individually, and in a church building associated with the person being ordained. Regardless, a few preparations need to be made. Provision should be provided for the ordinand(s) to kneel, either at the chancel rail (if a group) or at a prie-dieu (if one or two ordinands), and preparations must be made for the celebration of the eucharist with many communicants (see chapter 6). The stoles that are presented are usually carried and cared for by the sponsors.

Red, the color of the church, is the color for ordination (paraments, stoles, chasubles, copes, and so forth).

INSTALLATION OF A PASTOR

An optional element in the rite of installation for a pastor is for the pastor to be presented with signs of his or her calling: (a baptismal shell [if such are to be used]), a Bible, and a chalice and paten. When this option is used, the items are placed on a credence table before the service. After the presentation, the shell is placed on or near the font, the Bible is placed on the pulpit/ambo, and the chalice and paten are placed on the altar in preparation for the offertory.

DEDICATION OF WORSHIP FURNISHINGS

The rite for dedicating or blessing new worship furnishings such as a cross or crucifix, candles or candlesticks, sacramental vessels, paraments, funeral pall, a pall for an ossuary, oil, stained glass windows, chairs, and so forth—is set within the Holy Communion liturgy, just prior to the offertory prayer. When the offering (bread, wine, and money) is brought forward, the items to be dedicated may also be carried forward. A funeral pall, chasuble, or cope may be placed over the chancel rail for the dedication, and then removed for the remainder of the liturgy. After the service, the new items may be displayed by the altar guild. The altar guild or sacristan cooperates with the pastor in preparing the furnishings for their dedication.

Other special rites for dedicating the church building, an organ or other musical instrument, a facility for church use, and a cemetery, as well as a general order of blessing for other occasions may also be celebrated. For dedicating a columbarium or memorial garden, the rite for a cemetery dedication may be modified appropriately. For dedicating a new baptismal font or an altar, use the relevant sections of the rite for dedication of a church building. These rites themselves and respective "Notes on the Liturgy" within the orders of worship often provide instructions for altar guild preparations.

8. TIMES

Jesus Christ is the same yesterday and today and forever.
–(Hebrews 13:8)

I will bless the LORD at all times;
his praise shall continually be in my mouth.
–(Psalm 34:1)

In Judaism and from the beginnings of Christianity, prayer and worship have been organized around daily and yearly cycles. For altar guilds and sacristans, both daily prayer rites and the celebration of the church year take special preparations.

DAILY PRAYER

It is part of Old Testament as well as ancient Christian tradition to pray corporately (that is, together as the *corpus* or body of Christ) at certain hours of the day. The principal hours for prayer are morning and evening, the times of transition between light and darkness. In our time, many congregations use Morning Prayer and/or Evening Prayer on weekdays during Advent and Lent, and Morning Prayer is sometimes used on Sundays when the eucharist is not celebrated. Morning and Evening Prayer may be prayed in a simple fashion, or in an augmented form on Sundays and festivals.

The daily prayer services do not center about the altar, since they do not involve the celebration of the eucharistic meal. Instead, the heart of the daily prayer rites is the reading of scripture. Accordingly, these services center on a reading desk, which may be flanked with a tall candle on each side. If the nave has flexible seating, the chairs may be arranged in facing rows, with the reading desk at one end.

The traditional vestments for daily prayer leaders, clergy or lay, are cassock and surplice. An alb may be substituted. The stole is not worn unless there is a sermon, and then the stole is only worn by the ordained pastor who is preaching.

For festive daily prayer services, it is traditional for the principal leader (whether lay or clergy) to wear a cope, an ornate cloak or cape that is worn over the surplice or alb, is open in the front, and fastened near the neck with a clasp (known as a morse). The cope is worn in the appointed liturgical color for the day or season.

MORNING PRAYER Morning Prayer, also known as *Matins,* gives glory to God for the resurrection, symbolized by the light of the new day.

In preparation for this service, the reading desk is put in its place (see above) and a Bible is placed on it with the readings marked.

On Sundays, particularly during the seven weeks of Easter, the Paschal Blessing may conclude Morning Prayer. Because it is a remembrance of baptism and is thus a celebration of Easter, the Paschal Blessing may be led from the font. Water is placed in the font before the service. At the conclusion of the Paschal Blessing the leader may sprinkle the congregation with water from the font, using an evergreen bough. The sprinkling (known as *asperges*) is a traditional Christian remembrance of baptism. When this rite is used, the altar guild needs to place a fresh evergreen bough near the font before the service. Depending on the size of the congregation, the bough may be about one to two feet long, and longer needles work better than short ones. Needles toward the end of the bough cut from the trunk may need to be trimmed off with a knife in order to be picked up easily by the worship leader. It may be helpful to wrap about five inches of the branch with masking tape in order to gain an easy grasp on the branch without getting sap on the hand. It is also helpful for the entire branch to be rinsed clean with water in advance of the service.

EVENING PRAYER Also known as *Vespers,* Evening Prayer is a service of darkness and light, contemplation, scripture readings, and prayer. It derived from the ancient practice of lighting lamps at sunset, and the initial emphasis in Evening Prayer is Christ as the light of the world. This emphasis is enhanced dramatically when Evening Prayer begins after sunset with a procession in which a large unadorned lighted candle (known as the *lucernarium* candle or Evening Prayer candle) is carried into the darkened nave. This candle may be as large as a paschal candle (or nearly so), but the paschal candle itself should never be used for Evening Prayer; the two candles have different symbolism (see chapter 2). In preparation for the procession with light, the altar guild places a stand for the candle in the center of the chancel or in the midst of the congregation. At festive times of the year (particularly on festivals of light such as Christmas, the Epiphany, the Transfiguration, and Easter), the congregation may be given hand candles for lighting during the singing of the *Phos hilaron,* "Joyous light of glory." Preparations need to be made by the altar guild for the distribution, safe use, and collection of the hand candles. (See the section on hand candles, under "Other Candles," in chapter 2.)

The traditional evening psalm is Psalm 141, and because of the text, incense is appropriate during its singing: "Let my prayer rise before you as incense." Incense is an historic symbol of prayer ascending to God. In addition, incense is a visible reminder that our sinfulness is covered with Christ's righteousness. Incense may be used in various ways. The most modest is to place some burning sticks of incense in a bowl which is filled with sand; the container may be placed near the stand in which the Evening Prayer candle will be set. Another option is to light two or three pieces of charcoal in a thurible before the service, then during Psalm 141, two or three spoonsful (depending on the size of the worship space and the amount of incense desired) of incense are sprinkled on the charcoal, and one of the worship leaders then incenses the candle, the Bible, the altar, the other worship leaders, and the congregation. When this procedure is used, the altar guild places the stand for the thurible unobtrusively near the front of the worship space, puts the boat (the container for the incense) and spoon nearby, and prepares the thurible and charcoal. After the service, the charcoal is disposed of safely, and the thurible, stand, boat, and spoon are stored in the sacristy.

A prie-dieu may be used for the litany in Evening Prayer. It may be placed in front of the chair for the leader of the litany. Provision may be made for kneeling for the other worship leaders.

PRAYER AT THE CLOSE OF THE DAY *Compline,* as this service is traditionally known, is a simple and quiet rite of prayer and meditation. No special arrangements are needed for it, beyond the placement of the reading desk and its candles.

THE LITURGICAL YEAR

The church year is a wonderful way in which we recall and celebrate the mighty acts of God in history and in our own lives and times. It is a reminder of God's constant activity—not only God's interventions into human history, but also God's grace-filled activity among us now. Through the liturgical year we realize more and more deeply that we are a part of God's ongoing saving and loving activity.

For many centuries the church year calendar has shaped our worship: the readings, the sermons, the hymns and other music, the color of the paraments, and the appearance of worship space. Through a rich observance of the church year, each season and festival can make its fullest impact on the assembled congregation. The church is the grateful recipient and careful steward of the liturgical year. Faithful observance of it is both a privilege and a responsibility. In its ministry of preparation, it is important for the altar guild to study the background and significance of the various liturgical seasons and festivals. Each day of the church year has its own unique character and message, determined by the appointed readings for the day. Close attention to these readings enables us to celebrate the events in the life of our Lord and in church history with meaning.

The church year basically consists of two parts. The first half recalls and celebrates the life, death, and resurrection of Christ. This is the festival half of the year, and it has two divisions of its own. The Christmas cycle consists of the seasons of Advent, Christmas, and Epiphany. During this time the church focuses on the prophecies and events surrounding the incarnation. The Easter cycle is composed of the seasons of Lent and Easter, from Ash Wednesday through the Day of Pentecost. During these weeks we prepare for and observe the events surrounding our Lord's passion, death, and resurrection, and his sending of the Holy Spirit.

The second half of the church year is a more ordinary, non-festival time. It is the season *after* Pentecost (note that it is not the season *of* Pentecost), and is known as the Time of the Church. This season begins with the Holy Trinity (First Sunday after Pentecost) and concludes with the festival of Christ the King (Last Sunday after Pentecost). During these weeks the church concentrates on Christ's public ministry—his sermons, parables, and miracles. It is a time of growth in faith, hope, and love—and thus green paraments are used as a symbol of this growth.

Principal festivals of the church year are Easter Day, the Ascension of Our Lord, the Day of Pentecost, the Holy Trinity, Christmas Day, and the Epiphany of Our Lord. Interspersed throughout the year are days of special devotion, lesser festivals, commemorations, days commemorating events in church history, and other occasions.

For a summary of the seasons, festivals, and colors of the church year, see appendix A, p. 113.

ADVENT Advent consists of the four weeks before Christmas. The name of this first season of the liturgical year comes from a Latin word that means "coming." Advent focuses on this "coming" in three ways: the infant Jesus coming in the past—two millennia ago in Bethlehem, Christ coming in the present in word and sacraments and in the fellowship or communion of the church, and Christ coming again in the future at the end of time. In Advent we prepare for the celebration of Christ's coming in the incarnation, but more importantly we prepare for his second coming, when he will make all things new and judge the world in righteousness.

The preferred color for Advent is blue, the color of hope. The alternate color is purple, the royal color of the coming King. Blue, however, helps make apparent the major thematic differences between Advent and Lent. The blue used for Advent is royal blue, not pale or navy blue.

One of the themes of Advent is darkness, and it is thus appropriate to use fewer candles during these four weeks. That it is also a season of waiting may be reflected by simplifying the worship space, allowing the "festive look" to be reserved for Christmas and Epiphany. If there are skilled banner makers in the parish, however, a set of simple, dignified banners of the "O Antiphons" might be sewn and displayed in the worship space or narthex during Advent. These are especially appropriate and traditional during the last week of Advent and help stem the rush to putting up Christmas decorations.

The Advent wreath, which originated in home use in Europe after the Reformation, is a wreath on which four candles are placed, representing the four weeks of waiting during Advent. It may be suspended from the chancel ceiling or placed on a stand, usually near the gospel side of the altar (the left side as one faces the altar from the nave). The candles may be blue or purple, or even white. The former practice of three purple candles and one pink candle (which was lighted on Gaudete, former name of the third Sunday in Advent) no longer reflects the current lectionary and calendar, and should be avoided. If Advent wreaths are used, it is preferred that the wreath section be covered in real evergreens (which may need to be replaced halfway during the four weeks of Advent to lessen the danger of fire). A fire extinguisher should be kept close but out-of-sight in case of a fire.

It is neither traditional nor appropriate to put a so-called Christ candle in the center of the Advent wreath for Christmas (and the paschal candle is never properly used for such a purpose)—for the altar candles themselves represent Christ. On the first Sunday in Advent, the first candle is lighted during the psalm following the first reading. Another possibility for the lighting of the Advent wreath is during the gathering rite—perhaps at the time of the entrance hymn or the Kyrie. It seems even more preferable here, for the obvious connections between entering and the Lord's coming. On the second Sunday in Advent, the first candle is lighted prior to the service, and the second candle is lighted during the service. An additional candle is thus lighted during each Sunday in Advent until all four are lighted. The Advent wreath is used only for the four weeks in Advent, and is removed prior to all Christmas liturgies. The candles should be new each year to clearly indicate the passage of time.

Advent is a time for visual restraint and simplicity. It is appropriate to omit altar flowers during these weeks of preparation and waiting, in order to provide a marked contrast with the festivity and fulfillment of Christmas. When there are no flowers, vases are removed from the chancel and stored in the sacristy.

Advent should not be confused with Christmas. Christmas decorations, such as a Christmas tree, should not appear during Advent.

CHRISTMAS Christmas is the festive celebration of the Nativity of our Lord, the Word made flesh. This celebration of the incarnation lasts for twelve days—from Christmas Eve through Epiphany Eve.

The liturgical color for Christmas is white, symbolizing the light and purity of Christ and our great joy at his birth. White is used for the twelve days of Christmas, except for the festivals of St. Stephen (December 26) and of the Holy Innocents (December 28), when red is used in observance of their martyrdom.

Greens and wreaths may be placed in the nave and narthex, and at the entrance to the church building. The chancel may be adorned with abundant poinsettias, evergreen boughs mixed with branches of winter berries, and other flowers and potted plants. Plants, however, are never placed on the altar itself, nor should it be obstructed by decorations. If there is sufficient room, a Christmas tree (never artificial) may be set up. The tree may be bare or decorated with white lights and perhaps chrismons. If lights are used, the tree should be made fireproof, and local fire regulations must be observed. Chrismons (taken from the words "Christ monograms") are traditionally white and gold tree decorations fashioned by using various symbols for Christ. Chrismons may be made by the altar guild or other members of the parish.

Decorations for Christmas should not be put up until after worship on the fourth Sunday in Advent, because early decorating robs both Advent and Christmas of their full meaning.

For Christmas Eve, luminaria (paper bags weighted with sand and each containing a lighted white candle) may be placed along the entryways to the church building. It is a lovely Mexican tradition that can be used in any climate unless there is hard rain or heavy snow.

Luminaria

Especially for Christmas Eve services, and if local fire laws permit, candles may be placed in windows of the nave and on the ends of pews as brilliant symbols of Christ, the light of the world. If hand candles are distributed to worshipers, all fire safety precautions should be taken. For example, the altar guild should be certain that fire extinguishers are charged and readily accessible by persons prepared to use them.

If the parish has one, a Christmas creche may be placed in the worship space or narthex, although it should not detract from the prominence of the altar and font. Likewise, the creche may be put up outside the main entrance to the church building, or in another prominent place on the church grounds. The figures may be carried in the entrance procession on Christmas Eve or Day and then placed in the creche. The figures of the magi should be reserved until Epiphany. During the season of Christmas, the magi may be placed near the rear of the nave or in the narthex, as a reminder of their journey to Bethlehem and of the relationship between Christmas and Epiphany. This practice can be especially educational for children in the congregation.

It is very important that the eucharist be celebrated at all Christmas services—for it is the way the Word becomes flesh in our own midst, just as it became flesh in the infant in Bethlehem. The altar guild needs to be prepared for large numbers of communicants at Christmas liturgies and should have adequate supplies of bread and wine on the offertory table and/or credence, and an ample number of purificators on the credence.

EPIPHANY The Epiphany of our Lord is celebrated each year on January 6, marking the manifestation of Christ to the whole world. The coming of the magi to Bethlehem is reported in the gospel reading for this festival; this event may be made vivid by adding the figures of the magi to the creche during the entrance procession. Figures of the shepherds and perhaps the animals may be removed in advance.

White is the appointed color for Epiphany, a reminder that it is a festival of the light of Christ. It is also a festival in which abundant candles could be used to emphasize Christ as the light of the world.

On Epiphany Eve or following the Epiphany Day liturgy, there may be a ceremony of the burning of the greens, after the altar guild and helpers remove the greens from the church (interior and exterior). This may take place in the church parking lot or another safe place. Municipal permission and/or stand-by fire protection may be necessary.

THE EPIPHANY SEASON The first and last Sundays after the Epiphany are festivals. The second through the eighth Sundays after the Epiphany use green paraments as a symbol of our growth in knowing Jesus as God's Son and the Savior of the whole world and all its people.

THE BAPTISM OF OUR LORD The first Sunday after the Epiphany is the Baptism of Our Lord, in observance of Jesus' baptism by St. John the Baptist in the Jordan River. This Sunday also commemorates, in his baptism, Jesus' designation as the Son of God. Paraments for this day are white, since it is a festival of Christ. A baptismal festival may be held on this day (see chapter 5).

THE TRANSFIGURATION OF OUR LORD The Transfiguration of Our Lord is celebrated on the last Sunday after the Epiphany as a climax to the season and a prelude to Lent. Paraments for the Transfiguration are white.

ASH WEDNESDAY Since at least the seventh century, Ash Wednesday has been observed as the first day of Lent. This most penitential of days in the church year occurs between February 4 and March 10. The name is taken from the ancient tradition of placing ashes on the foreheads of penitents. In the biblical tradition, ashes represent God's condemnation of sin; human dependence on God for life; and humiliation and repentance. Ashes are also a reminder of death, for it is said as we are buried: "earth to earth, ashes to ashes, dust to dust."

Ashes for the imposition are made from palms from the previous year's observance of the Sunday of the Passion. The palms are cut into small pieces and burned (with rubbing alcohol or solid fuel firestarters, if needed). After an adequate quantity has been burned, work the ash through a fine wire mesh sieve. The ash may be mixed with a small amount of oil and placed in a small clay bowl or other container for the imposition. A lavabo bowl and towel will need to be provided for cleansing the minister's hands after the imposition of ashes. A small amount of fresh lemon juice or a few drops of liquid hand soap added to the water in the lavabo bowl will facilitate the cleansing.

Paraments for Ash Wednesday may be black (the color of ashes, humiliation, and mourning) or purple (the color of penitence). Black helps set the day apart from the rest of Lent and emphasizes the unique meaning of Ash Wednesday.

Flowers are not appropriate on Ash Wednesday, and the empty vases should also be removed from the chancel. If your parish is in a climate where it is still winter weather, bare branches (from deciduous trees, not coniferous trees) might replace the flowers as a reminder of Lent as a time of austerity. Other festive decorations, such as banners, are also removed. From Ash Wednesday through the Saturday of Holy Week, crosses, pictures, and statues may be removed or veiled with unbleached linen or purple fabric, as a demonstration that Lent is a time of austerity and purification. Holy Communion is celebrated on Ash Wednesday.

LENT Lent is the forty-day season of preparation for Easter. Traditionally, Lent has two primary themes—baptism and penitence—both in preparation for a worthy celebration of the paschal feast. Lent does not focus on our Lord's passion; that is the focus of Holy Week.

Paraments for Lent are purple, the color of penitence.

Flowers, being a symbol of joy, are appropriately omitted during Lent in order to help the congregation absorb the penitential character of the season. Empty vases, of course, are always removed from the chancel when not in use.

In some African American and other congregations, the Way of the Cross is observed on Fridays in Lent (but not on Good Friday). It consists of a procession that moves to stations consisting of a series of plain wood crosses on the walls of the worship space, or outdoors as a public witness. Visual depictions of the events being remembered may be adjacent to each cross; these may be of various artistic media and perhaps made by persons in the parish. The altar guild may oversee such preparations.

SUNDAY OF THE PASSION The first day of Holy Week is the Sunday of the Passion, also known as Palm Sunday. The mood of this day, reflecting its double name, is a mixture of triumph and tragedy. We observe both Christ's triumphant entry into Jerusalem as well as his death on the cross.

Paraments are scarlet, the dark red color of the crucifixion, and are used uniquely during most of Holy Week. The alternate color is purple, the penitential color of Lent. It is helpful to use scarlet, however, to distinguish Holy Week from the rest of Lent. Note that the darker scarlet (or crimson, as it is sometimes called) is not the same as bright red; red, the color of fire, is used for the Day of Pentecost and festivals of the church. Bright red is not used during Holy Week.

Palms may replace flowers in the chancel for this day. Other vases might hold pussy willows (but not in water) or forsythia—parishioners might be encouraged to cut and bring such branches from their own yards, and the altar guild can arrange them on Saturday afternoon before the Sunday of the Passion. If the climate is particularly cold, these branches might be brought indoors a few days or a week early to force blooming. However, the appearance of the worship space should not be too festive, and thus palm branches should be predominant over the flowers.

The altar guild is usually responsible for obtaining and preparing a sufficient quantity of palm branches for this day's procession. Actual palm *branches* serve the meaning of this day much more clearly than little crosses woven out of palms. Several palm branches should be saved and dried for making ashes for the following year's Ash Wednesday liturgy.

The presiding minister may wear a scarlet or purple cope during the entrance rite on the Sunday of the Passion.

MAUNDY THURSDAY Maundy Thursday recalls Jesus' example of loving service and his institution of the eucharist during the Last Supper in the upper room. The name of the day is from the Latin word *mandatum,* which means command. It refers to Jesus' words at the Last Supper, "I give you a new commandment, that you love one another. Just as I have loved you, you also should love one another" (John 13:34).

Paraments for Maundy Thursday are scarlet or white. Altar flowers are appropriate and should coordinate with the color of the paraments.

Holy Communion is always celebrated on Maundy Thursday. If your parish usually uses hosts (wafers), Maundy Thursday is a day to consider using real bread in order to emphasize the meal character of this sacrament (see chapter 6 for several eucharistic bread recipes).

A foot-washing ceremony, emphasizing Jesus' servanthood, is an optional part of the Maundy Thursday liturgy. A basin (large enough for two adult feet to fit easily); a large pitcher (perhaps a large ewer) of hot water (so that it is still warm by the time of the foot-washing); an apron, lavabo bowl, antibacterial soap, and several towels for the presiding minister; and a chair and towel for each participant need to be prepared before the service. The chairs and towels are usually put in place by the ushers just prior to the footwashing, but the altar guild or sacristans should be sure they are clean and in a convenient place prior to the service. Likewise, the pitcher may be filled with warm water and brought to the chancel (or front of the nave) as the chairs are being set up. For the water container, the congregation's ethnicity may be reflected by using, for examples, American Indian gourd vessels, or

African, Indian, or other Southeast Asian metal vessels. Ceramic vessels are heavy and prone to chip easily.

The presiding minister may wish altar guild members to be on hand to take the damp towels one-by-one to the sacristy, thus avoiding clutter in the worship space. Each towel should be used on only one person.

One of the sacristies should be prepared for the presiding minister to wash his or her hands thoroughly with soap after the footwashing (as the other items are being removed), to be prepared for the Holy Communion that follows.

At the conclusion of the Maundy Thursday liturgy, the altar is stripped in preparation for the austerity of Good Friday, and as a symbolic remembrance of Christ's humiliation by the soldiers. The altar guild may be asked to assist the presiding minister by carrying the eucharistic vessels, candles, ornaments, linens, paraments, and all other furnishings into the sacristy. It is helpful if the stripping of the chancel is rehearsed by all participants in advance. The sacristy should be clean and ready for all of these items. During the stripping of the altar, a cantor or the choir sings Psalm 22 and/or 88. The chancel and altar remain bare until the Easter Vigil. The altar guild, ministers, and remainder of the congregation leave the church in silence, contemplating prayerfully the solemn events of this truly awesome week.

Maundy Thursday is the first day of the Triduum, the three days of intense observance of the paschal mystery. Beginning with Maundy Thursday evening, the Triduum concludes Easter Evening. It is the most sacred and important time of the entire church year.

GOOD FRIDAY The original name of this day was probably "God's Friday." It is a day to celebrate the sacrifice on the cross of Christ, our Passover Lamb. The altar is bare of all linens and other furnishings. It is preferable for paraments to be omitted altogether on Good Friday, but if they are used, they should be scarlet or black. Flowers are not to be used on the very solemn day of Good Friday.

The Good Friday liturgy does not include the celebration of Holy Communion; this day's focus is the cross. The altar is not used at all during the Good Friday liturgy (except perhaps with the large cross; see below). Instead, the rite centers at one or more reading desks.

A large rough-hewn wooden cross may be prepared for the Good Friday liturgy. It may be placed in the narthex in readiness for its procession near the conclusion of the liturgy, or it may be placed in front of the altar (leaning against the altar or the communion rail—or, preferably, placed in a sturdy stand). A processional torch or another tall, lighted candle may be placed on a floor stand on each side of the cross.

During the veneration of the cross, it and the torches or candles may be held up by two assisting ministers.

If the service of Tenebrae is used, the altar guild will need to prepare a triangular candelabrum known as the Tenebrae hearse. Candles are extinguished individually following the reading of each psalm, representing humankind falling away from Christ. The paschal candle is not used in Tenebrae; it is reserved for Easter itself.

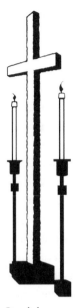

VIGIL OF EASTER The Easter Vigil is the most dramatic liturgy of the year, the climax of all of our spiritual preparations during Lent and Holy Week. It is a liturgy filled with contrasts between light and darkness, freedom and bondage, life and death. The Easter Vigil liturgy consists

Rough-hewn cross in floor stand

of four parts: Service of Light, Service of Readings, Holy Baptism, and Holy Communion.

Easter preparations are made with white paraments and multicolored flowers. Linens and ornaments that had been removed on Maundy Thursday are now replaced. An often-practiced alternative to advance placement of the flowers is having altar guild members (and perhaps others, but all of whom should be rehearsed well) bring in the flowers and plants during the singing of the "Gloria in excelsis" in the Vigil.

A large fire may be built in a brazier or on the ground outside the church building, in preparation for the lighting of the paschal candle. If such a fire is not feasible, a flame may be struck from flint and steel, an action that should be practiced in advance.

The paschal candle leads the Easter Vigil procession, and its stand should be placed in readiness near the center approach to the altar. A new paschal candle is normally acquired each year for this service. A cross, the Greek letters *alpha* and *omega,* and numerals of the current year are inscribed on the candle before the service.

Traditionally the presiding minister, while inscribing the candle, says the words "Christ yesterday and today [cross]; the beginning and the end [*alpha* and *omega*]; his are all times [2] and all ages [0]; to him be glory and dominion [0], through all the ages of eternity [1]. Amen." Grains of incense are placed in readiness near the candle stand, for insertion during the Easter Proclamation.

The candle is then lighted and carried in procession into the darkened church as the assisting minister intones, "The light of Christ," and the congregation responds, "Thanks be to God." Grains of incense and five wax nails (representing the five wounds of Christ) may be inserted into the cross at the appointed time during the Easter Proclamation in the Vigil. The incense reminds us that behind each nail of the crucifixion is the sweetness of our redemption.

Paschal candle

Four to twelve biblical readings are used in the vigil, and they should be marked in the Bible by the altar guild/sacristans for the convenience of the lectors.

The usual preparations are made for Holy Baptism (see chapter 5). Even if Holy Baptism is not actually celebrated at the Easter Vigil, the renewal of baptismal vows will occur, and the font should be filled with water, or a filled ewer may be placed near the font. An evergreen bough for sprinkling may be placed near the font for use during the renewal of baptismal vows (see suggestions for the preparation of an evergreen bough in one of the previous sections on Morning Prayer). If your parish does not have a large font that accommodates adult immersion or submersion (see chapter 5), it is relatively easy and inexpensive to construct a temporary one for the Easter Vigil. Cement blocks placed in the shape of a cross and doubly lined with heavy-duty plastic or rubber work well. See For Further Help, p. 130, for resources with instructions.

The usual preparations are also made for the eucharist (see chapter 6). Consider using a whole loaf of raised bread as a symbolic reminder of our Lord's resurrection.

The vigil begins in darkness, or preferably, outside the nave so there can be a procession of the whole congregation led by the paschal candle into the nave. Worshipers may carry small candles of their own (if local fire codes permit). The paschal candle is lit first, then the flame is passed to all worshipers' candles. The worship space may be decorated with flowers abundantly in advance, and left in place through at least part of the season of Easter. Flowering plants such as hydrangeas last several weeks, while those such as tulips do not. An abundance of flowers may be placed on and around the paschal candle stand.

EASTER The festival of the Resurrection of Our Lord is the queen of all Christian festivals, and all preparations for its celebration should make its unique significance apparent. All of the furnishings and appointments should be thoroughly cleaned and polished. The best linens should be used, and they should be spotlessly white and newly ironed. Gold paraments may be used on Easter Day (to emphasize the uniqueness of Easter Day, gold is reserved uniquely for this one single day of the church year; it is not even used for the Easter Vigil); white paraments are used during the rest of the Easter season. All paraments and vestments should be cleaned and ironed in preparation for the Easter celebration.

There should be more flowers for Easter Day than for the Easter Vigil—those in place from the vigil can simply be augmented. White or gold flowers are appropriate, and abundant Easter lilies and other flowers (including forsythia, lilac branches, blooming azaleas, branches of fruit blossoms, or whatever flowers are in season in your area at the time) may be used to adorn the worship space. Flowers and plants, however, are never placed on the altar itself. All decorations should serve to direct worshipers' attention to the altar, the paschal candle, the font, and the pulpit/ambo. The paschal candle in its floor stand is placed near the gospel side of the altar (the left side as one faces the front of the altar). It is lighted for all worship services from Easter Eve through the Day of Pentecost, as a reminder of the unity of these great fifty days of celebration.

Easter Day occurs between March 22 and April 25. The Easter celebration lasts for fifty days, and it is appropriate to have abundant flowers in the chancel throughout the season (replacing them with fresh flowers as necessary).

The eucharist should never be excluded from any Easter liturgy, since Easter is the paschal *feast*. The altar guild will need to prepare for large numbers of communicants, having adequate supplies of bread and wine, and purificators ready for use (see chapter 6).

THE ASCENSION OF OUR LORD The festival of the Ascension is forty days after Easter, and it celebrates Christ's triumphant ascension from the Mount of Olives to heaven. White paraments are used, and white flowers are fitting.

In former years, the paschal candle was often extinguished at the reading of the gospel on Ascension Day. However, it is more meaning-ful to allow the candle to burn through the eucharist on the Day of Pentecost, to stress the unity of the whole season of Easter. Regardless of when it is extinguished, the paschal candle is moved after the liturgy on the Day of Pentecost to its place near the font (where it is lighted only for baptisms or funerals).

THE DAY OF PENTECOST   The Day of Pentecost occurs fifty days after Easter. It celebrates the time when the Holy Spirit descended to the believers gathered in Jerusalem. It is, therefore, a day when decorations and ceremonies should be reminders of the Spirit.

Bright red paraments are used on the Day of Pentecost, reminders of the fire of the Spirit. Red gladioli are good this day for altar flowers, since their shape suggests tongues of fire. To emphasize the importance of this major festival, the chancel and worship space as a whole may be adorned with red geraniums and/or other red flowers. They should be arranged to call attention to the altar, font, and pulpit/ambo, although plants and flowers are never placed on the mensa of the altar. Follow-ing Pentecost worship services, geraniums and some other plants may be planted on the church grounds.

Pentecost is an appropriate day for full and festive processions, and banners may be made in preparation for the procession. Abun-dant bells may be attached to the banners to add a joyous note to the day. In advance of the celebration, the altar guild needs to put in place (in the narthex, or around the perimeter of the worship space) floor stands for the banners; the worship space should not look cluttered, and the banners are principally for the outdoor pro-cession. The presiding minister may wear a bright red cope for the Pentecost procession. The processional cross leads the procession, followed by the paschal candle (if the parish has a wind protector for it, in order to keep it lighted); these and other items are pre-pared in advance by the altar guild. Holy Communion is normally celebrated on this festival, and the altar guild will make the usual preparations (see chapter 6).

Since the Day of Pentecost is an appropriate time for Holy Baptism as well as for Affirmation of Baptism (Confirmation), the altar guild should seek advance instructions from the pastor (see chapter 5).

The paschal candle is extinguished after the final eucharist on this festival. After the service the paschal candle is moved to its place near the baptismal font (where it is lighted only for baptisms and placed near the coffin and lighted for funerals; see chapter 7).

THE SEASON AFTER PENTECOST   Except for festivals, Sundays after Pentecost use green paraments as a reminder that this is a season of spiritual growth.

THE HOLY TRINITY   This festival occurs on the First Sunday after Pentecost, celebrating the doctrine of the Trinity, one God in three persons. Paraments are white.

REFORMATION DAY   Reformation Day occurs on October 31, but it may be observed on the Sunday preceding that date. It is a day for giving thanks for Martin Luther and the other reformers, but much more, it calls attention to the ongoing need for the ecumemical growth and renewal of the church. Paraments are bright red, the color of the church.

ALL SAINTS DAY   This festival commemorates all the baptized people of God who have died in the faith. All Saints Day is November 1, but it may be observed on the Sunday following that date. The liturgical color is white. The altar guild might arrange a display in the narthex of photos and mementoes of parishioners and family members who have died in the past year. Following the liturgy of the day, there might be a procession to the parish cemetery if it is nearby, or columbarium, or memorial garden (see chapter 7); the altar guild can assist by having the processional cross and torches prepared.

This is also an appropriate day to dedicate a columbarium or memorial garden (adapting the Dedication of a Cemetery, *Occasional Services* p. 180 ff), if the congregation has installed one during the past year, and the altar guild/sacristans can assist with preparations of the cross, processional torches, and perhaps banners.

DAY OF THANKSGIVING   Although it is a civil agrarian rather than a religious holiday, it has become common for churches in North America to hold worship services on Thanksgiving Eve or Day. The liturgical color is white. Restrained decorations of the fruits of the earth—such as grapes, sheaves of grain, ears or stalks of corn—are appropriate, but should not draw attention away from the altar.

Since the word *eucharist* comes from the Greek word for *thanksgiving,* it is fitting to celebrate Holy Communion at Thanksgiving. Real, raised bread rather than wafers may be used, as may homemade grape wine, as reminders that God uses the fruits of the earth for God's gracious purposes. Ethnic types of bread may be used, but it should remain wheat bread.

CHRIST THE KING   The last Sunday after Pentecost celebrates the sovereignty or kingship of Christ and is so named. The liturgical color is white.

9. ORGANIZATION

For as in one body we have many members, and not all the members have
the same function, so we, who are many, are one body in Christ, and individually we are members one of another. We have gifts that differ according
to the grace given to us....
–(Romans 12:4-6a)

To be effective servants of the congregation's worship life, an altar
guild or sacristans group needs to be organized in a way that facil-
itates its work. Criteria for membership (see chapter 1) and principles
of organization are established by the parish worship committee, and
are approved by the congregation council. A sample constitution is
included in appendix B, p. 117.

MEMBERSHIP

An important qualification for all members of the altar guild is a sense
of awe in the presence of the Holy God. This awe gives rise to the spirit
of reverence that is so essential to the altar guild's work. The ministry of
liturgical preparations is a high privilege for a Christian, and dedicated
altar guild members and sacristans will carry out their responsibilities
with awe, joy, gratitude, and love for their Lord. Tasks of the altar guild
are not a burden but a delight, not a duty but a high privilege. There is
no room in the altar guild for complaining or grumbling. If the work
cannot be done with joy and a sense of privilege, a replacement should
be sought.

Another important characteristic is humility. While it is necessary for
altar guild members to be skilled in various ways, each member is only
one among many servants of the liturgy. The privilege of serving God is
shared with other altar guild members, with presiding and assisting ministers, acolytes, ushers, choristers, ushers, and worship committee members. Large egos do not belong in this work. Humility enables the cooperative spirit that is vital in working with others who also serve the
liturgy.

Members of the altar guild should be communicant members of the congregation, regular in worship attendance, frequent in receiving Holy Communion, always willing to learn, and eager to give priority in the use of time to the altar guild. To a great degree, the worship life of the parish depends on the altar guild/sacristans, and those members should in turn be reliable, cooperative, and committed to their work. (There is nothing worse for a pastor than to arrive at the church on a Sunday morning only to discover that the altar guild member(s) responsible for preparing for the eucharist have forgotten. It has happened to this writer, who therefore believes reliability cannot be overstated.)

With the advice of the parish worship committee, the pastor invites selected persons to membership on the altar guild. While the guild should be open to new members, it may not always be wise to issue a public invitation for volunteers, since that could result in members who are ill-equipped by attitude or skill.

Altar guild membership should not be limited to women. Indeed, sacristans were originally men. Men can serve the church as well as learn much about worship through service in the altar guild. (Sometimes using the term *sacristans* as the name of the group will encourage more men to participate.) Often it works well to have couples serve as working teams. Youth also have a place in this ministry of liturgical preparations. It can be a significant experience in both learning and service to have youth who are preparing for confirmation to serve as junior members, with confirmed youth as associate members in the altar guild. Youth might be invited to assist their parents who are guild members.

Since the work of the altar guild involves liturgical knowledge and many skills, it may be helpful to have new or prospective altar guild members serve six to twelve months as apprentices, under the training and supervision of an experienced member. Each apprentice might be assigned a mentor, or (in larger parishes) a mentor in each area of responsibility. Full membership may be granted after the satisfactory completion of this training period.

If there are enough skilled and willing persons in the parish, membership may be rotating. Rotation not only involves more persons in worship preparation, but also prevents the altar guild from becoming a clique. Rotating membership, however, requires a serious and intensive ongoing training program, and careful coordination. In any event, membership should include persons with the various skills of sewing and needlework, flower arrangement, chancel decoration, laundering and ironing of linens and vestments, polishing worship ornaments, cleaning the chancel and its furnishings, scheduling committees or work teams, keeping financial records and ordering supplies, and planning and conducting meetings.

TRAINING

It is very important for members of the altar guild to know not only what to do, but also why. For example, it is important not only to know the proper liturgical color to be used for a given day, but also the meaning of that color and the reason for its use on that day or season. Study should be a part of every altar guild meeting (see chapter 10), but initial training is also vital. Education and training for membership should begin with the basic questions, What is worship? Who is God, and why do we worship God? History and theology are involved as members learn about the development and meaning of worship space, the church year, the liturgy, and the sacraments. The background and meaning of worship furnishings and practices, symbolism and colors, are taught. The meaning of Holy Baptism and Holy Communion, and of the elements and vessels involved in their celebration, should be covered thoroughly and reviewed regularly. The use and meaning of other appointments and practices is also important. What does the paschal candle symbolize? When is it lighted? Why is it placed at the font after the season of Easter? Why do we strip the altar on Maundy Thursday? Why do we use a funeral pall, and why is it white? These and many other questions should be covered regularly during altar guild meetings.

Training also involves the practical skills necessary in vesting the altar, preparing for the sacraments, cleaning the chancel appointments, arranging items needed for a liturgy, changing paraments, caring for linens and vessels, preparing for the various days in the church year, preparing for weddings, funerals, and other occasional services, and carrying out other responsibilities indicated by the pastor. In all of these tasks, however, it is important that altar guild members learn about and understand the meaning as well as receive the practical instructions about how to do them.

The pastor usually does much of the training. For new members there will usually be special training sessions. For all altar guild members, continuing education is carried out during the study periods at regular meetings of the guild. Information about these study sessions is provided in chapter 10 of this book.

INSTALLATION

As a way of recognizing the ministry of the altar guild or sacristans, members may be installed during a congregational worship service. A sample installation rite is provided in appendix C, p. 120. The installation is set within the liturgy for Holy Communion, between the offertory and the offertory prayer.

The installation may be held whenever new members have been trained and are admitted to the guild. It may be useful to schedule installation once each year.

OFFICERS

Competent and dedicated officers are essential to a well-functioning altar guild. The presiding officer (who may be called coordinator, president, or director; coordinator will be used here because it connotes working with a variety of other people in the guild and more widely in the parish) works closely with the pastor and the parish worship committee; the coordinator may be appointed by the pastor with the advice and approval of the worship committee and the congregational council, or be elected by the guild. The coordinator chairs meetings, assigns and supervises the work of the guild, submits annual budget requests to the parish worship committee, sees that supplies are ordered, and carries out plans and directions from the pastor and parish worship committee. The coordinator serves as a member of the parish worship committee. A written report of activities is provided by the coordinator to the congregational council for the annual report to the congregation.

Other officers may be elected by the altar guild members at an annual organizational meeting.

An assistant coordinator (or vice president or assistant director, depending on what term is used for the chief officer) presides at meetings when the coordinator is unable to attend. This second officer also assists the coordinator in the supervision of the altar guild or sacristans.

She or he attends meetings of the parish worship committee in the absence of the coordinator.

The secretary keeps a written record of meetings and schedules, notifies members of meetings and assignments, and keeps an inventory of supplies and appointments.

The treasurer is responsible for the altar guild's financial transactions and records. This officer assists the coordinator in preparing a proposed budget each year, and provides an annual written financial report to the congregation council for inclusion in the annual report to the congregation.

COMMITTEES

A simple way to organize the altar guild is into monthly committees. Each month, the members on that committee are responsible for all tasks.

Another way to organize is to divide the altar guild into several working committees (see below), and to have one or two members of each committee serve each month. Committee memberships may rotate each year, so that all members learn several phases of the work.

While the number and organization of committees will depend on the size and worship schedule of each parish, the following schema is adaptable to most parishes. (Adapted from Ralph R. Van Loon, *Parish Worship Handbook* [Philadelphia: Parish Life Press, 1979], 44–45.) The sample constitution in appendix B, p. 117, follows this organization; it may be amended easily for the other schema.

The housekeeping committee sees that the chancel is clean for each worship service (in cooperation with the church sexton), launders and irons the fair linen monthly or as needed, changes paraments as indicated by the church year calendar, replaces candles as necessary, cleans and polishes worship appointments as needed, and sees that the missal and other items needed by ministers and acolytes are properly placed for each worship service. (See chapter 4 for more information about these tasks.)

The eucharistic committee prepares the eucharistic vessels and elements prior to each liturgy. After the service, members of this committee clean and store the vessels, properly dispose of the remaining bread and wine, and launder and iron all communion linens. (See chapter 6 for details of these responsibilities.)

The baptismal committee is informed of each scheduled baptism or baptismal festival, determines what items are needed (baptismal candles, baptismal garments, chrism, and towels), prepares the font, prepares warm water in the font or ewer, and places needed items (including baptismal towel, baptismal candle, baptismal garment, and chrism) near the font. Following worship, if the water does not remain in the font at all times, it is disposed of reverently and the font is dried; vessels are removed to the sacristy. If the font has a cover, it is replaced. (See chapter 5 regarding baptismal preparations.)

The occasional services committee makes preparations for weddings, funerals, baptismal affirmation (or this may be cared for by the baptism committee), healing rites, and other occasional services. Alternatively, especially in a large parish, there could be subcommittees for the two major occasional rites, weddings and funerals. (Regardless of organization, see chapter 7.)

The vestments committee launders, irons, and mends all vestments for the ministers and acolytes as needed. Albs should be ironed (and perhaps laundered, especially in hot climates) after each wearing. This committee is responsible for the care of chasubles, stoles, and other vestments as necessary. (See chapter 3 for information about vestments.)

The flower committee works with others in parish leadership to determine when flowers will be arriving and from whom, and to determine what is to be done with the flowers after worship. This committee arranges the flowers (or works cooperatively with the florist or persons donating the flowers in assuring appropriate colors and arrangements) and has them in place at least thirty minutes before each service; removes flowers from vases after worship, cleans and dries the vases, and removes the vases to a storage place; oversees the distribution of the flowers to the sick and homebound; and oversees flower arrangements for weddings and funerals.

If linens, paraments, and/or vestments are sewn locally, there may also be a needlework committee for this work.

There might also be a church year decorations committee for enabling the worship space to be visually appropriate for the various festivals and seasons of the year. (See chapter 8.)

RELATIONSHIPS

Since worship is the central function of the church, many persons and groups share responsibility for it. Cooperation, communication, and mutual respect are crucial for the worship life of the parish. The altar guild is responsible for the ministry of liturgical preparations, but it shares its servanthood with others. Good working relationships are vital.

The pastor, by virtue of ordination, has primary responsibility for the ministry of worship leadership. The pastor not only presides when the family of God gathers to worship, but also helps lead others in understanding and carrying out their ministries. The pastor supervises the training and advises the altar guild. In turn, the members of the altar guild work closely with the pastor in preparing for worship services. The pastor and coordinators of volunteers in the congregation should always be alert to the talents and interests of parishioners in seeking new members for the altar guild.

The parish worship committee is involved in planning for worship and, in doing so, works closely with the pastor. This committee oversees the work of the altar guild, and the coordinator of the guild serves on this committee. When the committee's worship plans are approved by the congregation council, the altar guild is responsible for seeing that the necessary preparations are made. The altar guild's annual budget request is submitted to the worship committee.

All parish policies and practices are determined by the congregation council in cooperation with the pastor, and consistent with the theology and policies of the denomination. The altar guild has input into this process through its representation on the parish worship committee. Communications with the congregation council are normally made through the parish worship committee.

Acolytes also have an important role in parish worship. The official relationship between the altar guild and the acolytes will depend on the parish, but guild members should always stand ready to help and support acolytes. In most parishes, the altar guild is responsible for acolytes' vestments, and sometimes acolytes use one of the sacristies for vesting and pre-service preparations. Members of the altar guild will want to be sure that they set an appropriate example for acolytes in their attitudes, words, and actions.

The altar guild also needs a cooperative relationship with the church sexton. The pastor and congregation council, with the advice of the worship committee, determine the division of responsibilities between the sexton and the altar guild. Usually the sexton cleans the chancel floor and leaves other cleaning in the chancel to the altar guild.

10. MEETINGS

Jesus said to the disciples: "For where two or three are gathered in my name, I am there among them."
–(Matthew 18:20)

It is helpful for the altar guild to meet monthly, although in small congregations, bimonthly meetings may suffice. These regular meetings foster good communication, provide the opportunity for continual learning and spiritual growth, enable scheduling to occur and assignments to be made, provide for checks on members' accountability, and are a time for fellowship in the faith.

There may also be a need, particularly in larger congregations, for regular (quarterly, for example) meetings of at least some of the committees, if that is how the group is organized. (See chapter 9.)

AGENDA

Meetings are called to order by the coordinator. The agenda is usually set forth in the local altar guild/sacristans' constitution, but normally it includes the following items:

Call to order
Attendance
Devotions
Study
Officers' reports
Committee reports
Old business
New business
Prayer

As a part of new business, the coordinator reviews the worship schedule for the coming month(s) and makes assignments. Refreshments and fellowship may follow the business meeting.

Devotions and Prayer

Spiritual growth is very important for altar guild members and sacristans. Hence, opening devotions and closing prayer are an important part of the meetings. Members may take turns leading the group in devotions, and the pastor may suggest various rites to use. Possibilities for opening devotions from *Lutheran Book of Worship* include Responsive Prayer 1 (p. 161) or a simplified form of Morning Prayer (p. 131) for morning meetings; Responsive Prayer 2 (p. 164) for afternoon meetings; and Responsive Prayer 2 or a simplified form of Evening Prayer (p. 142) for evening meetings. The Litany (p. 168) could be used at any time, but it is especially appropriate for Lent. Opening devotions might also take the form of a spiritual reading.

All of the volumes listed here and in the For Further Help section, p. 130, should be in the parish and/or pastor's library; full citations are provided in For Further Help. To focus on the time of the church year, fine texts can be found in current or past issues of *Sundays and Seasons* (Augsburg Fortress, published annually), and in any of the *Sourcebook* series (for examples, *An Easter Sourcebook, An Advent Sourcebook*) published by Liturgy Training Publications. (It would be a worthy project to provide such volumes for the parish library if it does not already have them, and to provide information about them in the parish newsletter.)

If the meeting is on or near a lesser festival or commemoration, appropriate texts and prayers are included in *Festivals and Commemorations* by Philip Pfatteicher (Augsburg, 1980). Interesting information about the background and meaning of many hymn texts is available in *Hymnal Companion to the Lutheran Book of Worship* by Marilyn Kay Stulken (Fortress, 1981), and *With One Voice Reference Companion* (Augsburg Fortress, 2000). For brief, excellent devotional readings of a more general nature, see, for examples, *A Metaphorical God* by Gail Ramshaw (Liturgy Training Publications), or Martin Marty's insightful books on the sacraments, *The Lord's Supper* and *Baptism* (both Fortress Press).

If the meeting is held on (or to plan) a festival or commemoration of the church year, scripture and prayers should be selected accordingly. It is helpful to refer to the calendar in *Lutheran Book of Worship* (pp. 9–12), to *Readings and Prayers* (a small booklet published by Augsburg Fortress containing prayers for the day and readings according to the Revised

Common Lectionary), and to a comprehensive calendar such as that published annually by Ashby, which includes commemorations.

For other days, scripture readings may be selected from the Daily Lectionary in *Lutheran Book of Worship* (p. 179). Year One readings are used beginning in Advent preceding odd-numbered years. Year Two readings are used beginning in Advent preceding even-numbered years. Alternately, a table of daily lectionary readings related to the Sunday lectionary is found in *Between Sundays* (Augsburg Fortress, 1997). It can be very meaningful to combine devotions with study by reading and then discussing (perhaps with some "input" from the pastor) one or more of the appointed biblical readings for the day or festival or season for which preparations will be made at this meeting. A copy of the Revised Common Lectionary, in which the texts are printed out from the New Revised Standard Version is most helpful (see For Further Help, p. 130).

For closing devotions at evening meetings, immediately before members go home, Prayer at the Close of the Day (*LBW*, p. 154), also known as Compline, may be used. Because this brief office is the "going-to-bed prayer of the church," it should come at the conclusion of the meetings, following refreshments and fellowship.

The following prayers, from *Lutheran Book of Worship* and *Occasional Services,* may be used at the opening or closing of meetings:

Almighty God, we give you thanks that you provide for the work of your church through the different gifts of the members of this altar guild [sacristans group]. Help us to recognize and act upon every opportunity for service. Guide our diversity by your one Spirit, that everything we think, say, and do may be for the common good of your church; through your Son, Jesus Christ our Lord. Amen

God of majesty, whom saints and angels delight to worship in heaven: Be with your servants who make art and music for your people, that with joy we on earth may glimpse your beauty; and bring us to the fulfillment of that hope of perfection which will be ours as we stand before your unveiled glory. We pray in the name of Jesus Christ our Lord. Amen

Lord God of our salvation, it is your will that all people might come to you through your Son Jesus Christ. Inspire our witness to him, that all may know the power of his forgiveness and the hope of his resurrection. We pray in his name. Amen

Almighty God, by our baptism into the death and resurrection of your Son Jesus Christ, you turn us from the old life of sin. Grant that we who are reborn to new life in him may live in righteousness and holiness all our days, through your Son, Jesus Christ our Lord. Amen

Almighty God, draw our hearts to you, guide our minds, fill our imaginations, control our wills, so that we may be wholly yours. Use us as you will, always to your glory and the welfare of your people; through our Lord and Savior Jesus Christ. Amen

Direct us, O Lord, in all our doings with your most gracious favor and further us with your continual help, that in all our works, begun, continued, and ended in you, we may glorify your holy name and finally, by your mercy, obtain everlasting life; through Jesus Christ our Lord. Amen

Gracious Father, we pray for your holy catholic Church. Fill it with all truth and peace. Where it is corrupt, purify it; where it is in error, direct it; where in anything it is amiss, reform it; where it is right, strengthen it; where it is in need, provide for it; where it is divided, reunite it; for the sake of Jesus Christ, your Son our Savior. Amen

O most loving Father, you want us to give thanks for all things, to fear nothing except losing you, and to lay all our cares on you, knowing that you care for us. Protect us from faithless fears and worldly anxieties, and grant that no clouds in this mortal life may hide from us the light of your immortal love shown to us in your Son, Jesus Christ our Lord. Amen

Watch, dear Lord, with those who wake or watch or weep, and give your angels charge over those who sleep. Tend the sick, rest the weary, bless the dying, soothe the suffering, pity the afflicted, shield the joyous. In your love, give us all this, through Jesus Christ our Lord. Amen

TOPICS FOR STUDY

The competence of the altar guild depends on good study sessions at the meetings. Included may be demonstrations of specific tasks; slides or videos on symbols, architecture, the sacraments, liturgy, and the church year; and programs presented by the pastor, members, or guests. The list of possible topics is almost endless and includes the following:

Contents of *Lutheran Book of Worship* (including *LBW* Ministers edition)

Contents of *Occasional Services*
Contents of *This Far by Faith* or *Libro de Liturgia y Cántico*
Meaning of Holy Communion
Meaning of Holy Baptism
Meaning of Morning Prayer
Meaning of Evening Prayer
Meaning of Prayer at the Close of the Day
Church architecture and its symbolism
Development and structure of the church year
Meaning and customs of seasons and festivals
Meaning of parts of the eucharistic liturgy
Meaning of the burial liturgy
Meaning of the marriage liturgy
Old Testament worship
New Testament worship
Worship in the early church
Luther and worship
Worship in its cultural context(s)
Development and meaning of vestments
Meaning of liturgical colors
Worship furnishings and appointments
Symbols
Meaning and use of candles in worship
Eucharistic vessels and elements
Church art
Music and/or Hymns in worship
Psalms in worship
Meaning of the sign of the cross
Meaning of the exchange of the peace
Rubrics (now often called "Notes on the Liturgy")

The For Further Help section (p. 130) includes resources that will be useful in preparing study programs. If your parish library does not include these books, perhaps the altar guild could purchase them as gifts for the library. The pastor may also have suggestions for study sessions.

With regard to resources both for devotions and for study, it is important to be aware that many of the "spiritual" books sold in bookstores present theology that is unacceptable for Lutherans and many other mainline denominations.

Other possibilities for learning include visits to other churches to observe their worship space, furnishings, sacristies, paraments, and vestments. The synod worship committee may be able to suggest good places to visit. In addition, the parish worship committee chairperson or parish musicians may be invited to altar guild meetings to discuss their work in planning and preparing for worship. A local florist could come to discuss the care and arrangement of flowers. An architect or ecclesiastical artist might discuss the role of art and architecture in worship.

Joint meetings with the altar guild/sacristans of other parishes—even of other denominations—can be jointly enriching. Many of the study ideas listed above could be the focus of joint ecumenical meetings, and it is important that differences as well as similarities of practice and understanding be recognized and respected. Likewise, joint meetings with congregations representing other ethnic and/or cultural traditions can be good learning experiences, particularly if one's own parish is multi-ethnic or multicultural. Many ideas can be obtained through ecumenical and multi-ethnic meetings, but be careful not to "pick and choose" worship practices or artistic forms without fully understanding their origins, background, and meaning, and do not trivialize them (for doing so shows lack of respect for the people whom they represent). A good perspective to keep in mind *and heart* regarding ecumenical and cultural sharing is: "As many of you as were baptized into Christ have clothed yourselves with Christ. There is no longer Jew or Greek, there is no longer slave or free, there is no longer male and female; for all of you are one in Christ Jesus" (Galatians 3:27-28).

PROJECTS

Members of the altar guild might undertake special projects from time to time, including some of the following:

1. Accompany the pastor on communion visits to homebound persons. If parish practice involves lay members taking the communion to the sick and homebound after Sunday morning worship, altar guild members could be involved in this ministry.

2. Exhibit and discuss linens, paraments, vessels, and vestments at confirmation classes, adult classes, worship committee meetings, church council meetings, and women's and men's meetings.

3. Discuss with the pastor the possibility of assisting first communion classes.

4. Hold displays or exhibits of vessels, vestments, linens, paraments, and appointments in the narthex as a means of worship education for the parish.

5. Prepare articles for the parish newsletter on symbols and colors of the church year, or on the names and use of sacramental vessels, linens, and other worship accoutrements.

6. If the parish owns historic eucharistic vessels, they might be displayed as a part of an anniversary celebration.

7. Members skilled in needlework could make wedding cushions, new paraments, new vestments, new linens, a funeral pall, or an ash urn (ossuary) pall.

8. Make a set of chrismons for decorating the church Christmas tree; after they are made, a program on symbolism could be presented using the chrismons to illustrate the symbols. (Older children in church school could be enlisted to help with making chrismons.)

9. A calendar of liturgical festivals and commemorations, with suggested scripture readings and the appointed colors, could be procured or prepared for distribution or sale to the congregation. If sold, proceeds could be used for books for the sacristy or parish library, or for new items needed by the congregation, such as a processional cross, processional torches, small glass cruet for oil, paschal candle and stand, white funeral pall, ossuary pall, chasubles, copes, other new vestments, new linens or paraments, or a fund toward a free-standing altar or a baptismal pool that will accommodate adult submersion.

10. Make bread and/or wine for sacramental use. (See recipes in chapter 8.)

11. Offer to help church school teachers when lessons address worship, symbols, and the church year.

12. If a mission congregation is established in the region, offer assistance in organizing and training an altar guild or group of sacristans in the new congregation. Offer to give or make them a new liturgical item for their use.

13. Prepare a list of altar guild items that could be provided through memorial gifts.

APPENDIX A / OUTLINE OF THE CHURCH YEAR AND COLORS

Seasons and Principal Festivals

The Christmas Cycle
Advent Season
  Four Sundays in Advent (blue or purple)
Christmas Season
  The Nativity of Our Lord—Christmas Eve, Christmas Dawn, and Christmas Day (white)
  First and Second Sundays after Christmas (white)
Epiphany Season
  The Epiphany of Our Lord (white)
  The Baptism of Our Lord—First Sunday after the Epiphany (white)
  Second through Eighth Sundays after the Epiphany (green)
  The Transfiguration of Our Lord—Last Sunday after the Epiphany (white)

The Easter Cycle
Lenten Season
  Ash Wednesday (black or purple)
  First through Fifth Sundays in Lent (purple)
Holy Week
  Sunday of the Passion—Palm Sunday (scarlet or purple)
  Monday through Wednesday (scarlet or purple)
The Three Days
  Maundy Thursday (scarlet or white)
  Good Friday (no paraments)
  Vigil of Easter (white)
Easter Season
  The Resurrection of Our Lord—Easter Day (gold or white)
  Second through Seventh Sundays of Easter (white)

The Ascension of Our Lord (white)
The Day of Pentecost (red)

The Time of the Church
Season after Pentecost
   The Holy Trinity—First Sunday after Pentecost (white)
   Second through Twenty-seventh Sundays after Pentecost (green)
   Christ the King—Last Sunday after Pentecost (white)

LESSER FESTIVALS

Lesser festivals may have precedence over Sundays for which the color is green, and over the First and Second Sundays after Christmas.

November 30—St. Andrew, Apostle (red)
   First apostle to follow Jesus. Martyred at Patras in Greece on this date in A.D. 60.
December 21—St. Thomas, Apostle (red)
   One of the twelve apostles; was unwilling to believe in the resurrection until he had touched Jesus.
December 26—St. Stephen, Deacon and Martyr (red)
   One of the seven deacons ordained by the apostles. Was the first to die for his faith; martyred by stoning.
December 27—St. John, Apostle and Evangelist (white)
   With James and Peter, St. John was in the inner circle of the apostles. Was the only one of the apostles not to be martyred.
December 28—The Holy Innocents, Martyrs (red)
   The innocent young children of Bethlehem killed by King Herod in his attempt to destroy the infant Jesus.
January 1—The Name of Jesus (white)
   Recalls the circumcision and naming of Jesus.
January 18—The Confession of St. Peter (white)
   Celebrates St. Peter's confession that Jesus is "the Christ, the Son of the living God." Begins the Week of Prayer for Christian Unity.
January 25—The Conversion of St. Paul (white)
   Celebrates the conversion of Saul to Paul. Concludes the Week of Prayer for Christian Unity.

February 2—The Presentation of Our Lord (white)
Recalls the presentation of Jesus in the temple by his parents, and celebrates the occasion of the *Nunc dimittis,* the Song of Simeon. Also known as Candlemas, for the tradition of blessing candles on this day.

February 24—St. Matthias, Apostle (red)
St. Matthias was selected to fill the vacancy in the twelve apostles left by Judas Iscariot's death.

March 25—The Annunciation of Our Lord (white)
Observes the angel's announcement to Mary that she would give birth to Jesus.

April 25—St. Mark, Evangelist (red)
Companion of St. Peter; author of Second Gospel. Martyred in Alexandria in 64 A.D.

May 1—St. Philip and St. James, Apostles (red)
The remains of these two apostles were placed in the Church of the Apostles in Rome on this date in 561 A.D.

May 31—The Visitation (white)
Marks Mary's visit to Elizabeth, and celebrates the occasion of the *Magnificat,* the Song of Mary.

June 11—St. Barnabas, Apostle (red)
Early Christian disciple who worked with St. Paul; believed to have been martyred in Cyprus in 61 A.D.

June 24—The Nativity of St. John the Baptist (white)
Celebrates the birthday of St. John the Baptist.

June 29—St. Peter and St. Paul, Apostles (red)
Celebrates the apostles' ministry to both the Jewish and gentile world. Both are believed to have been martyred in Rome.

July 22—St. Mary Magdalene (white)
Principal witness of the resurrection.

July 25—St. James the Elder, Apostle (red)
Brother of St. John; the only apostle whose martyrdom is recorded in Scripture (Acts 12:2).

August 15—Mary, Mother of Our Lord (white)
Honors the mother of Jesus. Celebrated on the traditional date of Mary's death.

August 24—St. Bartholomew, Apostle (red)
One of the twelve apostles; traditionally believed to have been skinned alive.

September 14—Holy Cross Day (red)
Dates from the dedication in 335 A.D. of a basilica in Jerusalem, built by Constantine, on the site of the crucifixion and resurrection.

September 21—St. Matthew, Apostle and Evangelist (red)
Roman tax collector who became a disciple. Believed to have been martyred.

September 29—St. Michael and All Angels (white)
Honors the archangel Michael. Only festival of the angels retained by Luther; also known as Michaelmas.

October 18—St. Luke, Evangelist (red)
A gentile physician, follower of Christ, and companion of St. Paul; author of the Third Gospel and Acts.

October 28—St. Simon and St. Jude, Apostles (red)
Two apostles; martyred together in Persia.

October 31—Reformation Day (red)
Anniversary of Luther's posting of his Ninety-five Theses in Wittenberg, Germany, in 1517.

November 1—All Saints' Day (white)
Commemorates all the baptized people of God who have died in the faith.

Note: In addition to these lesser festivals, *Lutheran Book of Worship* also includes a full calendar of commemorations, with dates and appointed colors. Both *Libro de Liturgia y Cántico* and *This Far by Faith* suggest a number of additional commemorations; see those books for dates and information.

APPENDIX B / SAMPLE CONSTITUTION

A written constitution is helpful for any organization, providing consistency and good order over the years. The altar guild or sacristans' group constitution should be written with the help of the pastor, and it is subject to approval by the parish worship committee and the congregation council. The following is only a sample; it needs adaptation for actual usage, in order to reflect local organization. Regarding Article 4, it should be noted that a variety of nomenclature is possible, as are two ways of organizing the work; for details on these options, see chapter 9 and amend the constitution as desired locally.

Article 1—Name
The name of this organization is the Altar Guild [or Sacristans] of *(name of congregation)*.

Article 2—Purposes
1. To study and constantly grow in understanding, appreciating, and living the worship life of the church.
2. To care for the worship space, its furnishings, linens, vestments, paraments, appointments, and the sacramental elements and vessels.
3. To prepare the worship space for all liturgies and corporate rites, including Sunday worship.
4. To care for vestments of the pastor(s), lay assisting ministers, and acolytes.

Article 3—Membership
1. The membership shall consist of a minimum of *(number)* active communicant members of the parish, appointed by the pastor, and with the advice and approval of the parish worship committee and congregational council.
2. Membership is open to both women and men.

3. Pre-confirmation youth may serve as junior members, and confirmed youth may serve as associate members.

Article 4—Officers

1. The officers are: coordinator, assistant coordinator, secretary, and treasurer.
2. The coordinator is appointed annually by the pastor, with the advice of the parish worship committee and the approval of the congregation council [or: is elected annually by the guild/sacristans].
3. Other officers are elected by the guild for one-year terms.
4. The officers have the following duties:
   a) The coordinator presides at meetings; assigns and supervises the work of the guild; serves as a member of the parish worship committee; sees that plans and directions from the pastor, worship committee, and congregation council are carried out by the guild/sacristans; prepares a written report each year for the annual meeting of the congregation; and orders supplies as needed. The coordinator and the treasurer prepare the proposed budget each year, and the coordinator submits it to the parish worship committee. The coordinator prepares a written report each year for the annual meeting of the congregation.
   b) The assistant coordinator presides at meetings in the absence of the coordinator and assists the coordinator as requested.
   c) The secretary keeps a record of meetings and schedules, notifies members of guild meetings and service assignments, and keeps an inventory of supplies and worship appointments (advising the coordinator when orders need to be placed).
   d) The treasurer keeps financial records and provides a written financial report each year for the annual meeting of the congregation. The treasurer assists the coordinator annually in the preparation of the proposed budget.

Article 5—Committees

1. The standing committees are: housekeeping, Holy Communion, Holy Baptism, occasional services, vestments, flowers, needlework, and church year decorations/worship environment.
2. The housekeeping committee sees that the chancel is clean and prepared for all services, cares for the fair linen and paraments, replaces

candles, cleans and polishes worship appointments, and puts in place books and other needed items for services.

3. The Holy Communion committee prepares the altar for each celebration of the Holy Communion, and cares for the sacramental elements, vessels, and linens.

4. The Holy Baptism committee prepares the font/pool, water, and other necessary items for each baptism.

5. The occasional services committee prepares for weddings, funerals, healing rites, and other occasional rites of the church.

6. The vestments committee cares for all vestments for ministers and acolytes.

7. The flowers committee prepares and places all flowers in the chancel, cares for vases, and oversees the distribution of flowers to the sick and homebound.

8. The needlework committee oversees the making of paraments, vestments, linens, and other needlework items.

9. The decorations committee plans and oversees the placement of all seasonal decorations for the liturgical year.

Article 6—Meetings

1. The regular monthly meetings are on: _____.

2. The January [or other month] meeting is considered the annual meeting, during which the assistant coordinator, secretary, and treasurer are elected.

3. Special meetings may be called by the coordinator or the pastor. Members should be notified at least one week in advance.

4. The order of business at regular meetings is: call to order, attendance, devotions, study, officers' reports, committee reports, old business, new business, and closing prayer.

Article 7—Amendments

Amendments to this constitution may be made by a two-thirds vote of the altar guild members/sacristans, and must be ratified by the congregation council upon recommendation by the parish worship committee.

APPENDIX C / ORDER FOR INSTALLATION

This order, adapted from Occasional Services *(p. 143–5), follows the offering and the offertory in the Holy Communion liturgy.*

The presiding minister addresses the congregation:

Dear Christian friends: Baptized into the priesthood of Christ, we all are called to offer ourselves to the Lord of the church in thanksgiving for what he has done and continues to do for us. It is our privilege to recognize and support those who are engaged in the work of this congregation, especially those in the ministry of the altar guild [sacristy].

As a representative of the congregation reads a brief description (to be prepared in advance, perhaps using article 2 of the sample constitution provided in appendix B, p. 117) of the ministry of the altar guild/sacristy, the persons engaged in that ministry stand.

The presiding minister addresses those who are beginning (or beginning a new term) their ministry in the altar guild or sacristy group:

Having offered yourselves in the altar guild ministry of this congregation, will you follow our Lord's example of humble service?

The persons being installed respond:

Yes, with God's help.

The presiding minister says:

Let us pray. God of majesty, whom saints delight to worship in heaven and on earth: Bless the ministry of those serving in the altar guild [as sacristans], that we may know the joy of your presence and may worship to the glory of your holy name; through Jesus Christ our Lord.

The congregation responds: Amen

The presiding minister concludes:

For all who offer themselves in your name, we give thanks, O God. Give them the joy of service, and constant care and guidance. Help us all to be both willing servants and thankful recipients of ministry, that your name be glorified, your people live in peace, and your will be done; through Jesus Christ our Lord.

The congregation responds: Amen

The service continues with the offertory prayer.

GLOSSARY

For a comprehensive and practical dictionary of worship terms, see Van Loon and Stauffer, *Worship Wordbook,* cited in For Further Help, p. 130.

acolyte From the Greek for "to follow"; a lay liturgical assistant (often but not necessarily a youth) who serves in such various roles as crucifer, torchbearer, bannerbearer, bookbearer, candlelighter, and server.

Advent From the Latin for "coming"; the four weeks before Christmas which constitute the first season of the liturgical year.

Advent wreath A wreath with four candles, used during the four weeks of Advent.

Affirmation of Baptism Rite used for confirmation, reception of new members, and restoration to membership.

alb Full-length white vestment used in worship since the sixth century; usually worn with cincture. Worn by presiding and assisting ministers, acolytes, choristers.

alms basin Large plate or basket in which the smaller offering plates or baskets are received and carried in the offertory procession.

altar Table in the chancel used for the celebration of the Holy Communion. It is the central furnishing of the worship space.

altar rail Railing enclosing the chancel at which people stand or kneel to receive Holy Communion.

ambo Another (more historic) name for the pulpit, reading desk, or lectern.

amice (AH-miss) White linen cloth resembling a collar which may be worn with an alb.

ante-communion That portion of the Holy Communion liturgy preceding the great thanksgiving.

antependium Parament for pulpit and lectern.

apse The semicircular (or polygonal) projection or alcove at the end of the chancel in traditional church architecture.

Ascension Principal festival occurring forty days after Easter Day, celebrating Christ's ascension to heaven.

ashes Symbol of repentance and mortality used in the Ash Wednesday liturgy; made by burning palms from previous year.

Ash Wednesday First day of Lent; occurs between February 4 and

March 10. Name derives from the traditional practice of imposing ashes on worshipers' foreheads.

asperges (ah-SPUR-jess) Ceremony during the renewal of baptismal vows during the Easter Vigil, and during the paschal blessing in Morning Prayer, in which water from the font is sprinkled over the congregation as a remembrance of their baptism.

assisting minister Lay person who assists the ordained presiding minister in worship leadership.

baptism The sacrament of water and the Holy Spirit, in which we are joined to Christ's death and resurrection and initiated into the church.

baptistery The area in which the baptismal font is located.

Benedicite, omnia opera (benn-eh-DEECH-ih-tay, OHM-nee-ah OH-purr-ah) Latin title for the final canticle in the Easter Vigil, "All you works of the Lord, bless the Lord," from Song of the Three Young Men.

Benedictus (benn-eh-DIK-tus) Latin title for the gospel canticle "Blessed be the God of Israel," in Morning Prayer, from Luke 1:68-79.

black Liturgical color for Ash Wednesday; symbolizes ashes, repentance, and humiliation.

blue Liturgical color for Advent; symbolizes hope.

bobeche (BOH-besh) White plastic or cardboard drip protector for candles.

burse Square fabric-covered case in which the communion linens are often carried to and from the altar.

candlelighter Long-handled device used to light and extinguish candles.

candlestick Ornamental base holder for candle.

cassock Full-length black "undergarment" worn under surplice or cotta.

catechumen A person (usually an adult or older youth) preparing for Holy Baptism through a process of formation and special rites leading up to baptism at the Easter Vigil.

catechumenate The process for preparing adults and older youth for Holy Baptism, often culminating at the Easter Vigil. It is a process of growth in spirituality, worship, service, as well as learning, and is based on the practice of the early church.

censer Vessel in which incense is burned; also called thurible.

cerecloth (SEAR-kloth) Traditionally, with stone altars, the first cloth placed on the mensa; and hence usually made of wax-treated linen.

chalice Cup used for the wine in the Holy Communion.

chancel Elevated area where altar and pulpit/ambo are located.

chasuble (CHAH-zuh-bel) The principal vestment for the Holy Communion liturgy; worn like a poncho by the presiding minister over alb and stole.

chrism (krizm) From the Greek for "Anointed One," a title for Christ. Fragrant oil used for anointing in Holy Baptism.

chrismon (KRIZ-mohn) From the words "Christ monograms"; symbols of Christ often used to decorate Christmas trees.

chrisom (KRIS-om) White garment placed on a person after baptism as a symbol of being clothed in the righteousness and eternal life of Christ.

Christ the King The last Sunday of the church year, celebrating the kingship or sovereignty of Christ.

Christmas Principal festival of the church year which celebrates Christ's birth or nativity; also known as the Nativity of Our Lord.

ciborium (sih-BOR-ee-um) Tall covered vessel which holds wafers for the Holy Communion.

cincture (SINK-chur) Rope belt worn with an alb.

columbarium (KOLL-um-BARR-ee-um) Wall or other structure with niches for burial of ashes from cremation.

Compline (KAHM-plin) From the Latin for "complete," referring to the prayers which complete the day's worship. An order for night prayer used as the last worship service before bed. Also known as Prayer at the Close of the Day.

confirmation Liturgical form of Affirmation of Baptism, marking the completion of a period of instruction in the Christian faith. Used with youth who were baptized as infants.

cope Long cape worn by worship leader, lay or ordained, for certain processions and ceremonial occasions.

corporal Square white linen cloth placed on the center of the fair linen on the mensa, on which the eucharistic vessels are placed for the celebration of Holy Communion.

corpus Latin for "body." Carved figure of Christ attached to a cross; together, cross and corpus are a crucifix.

cotta (KOTT-ah) Short white vestment worn over cassock by acolytes and choir members (unless albs are worn).

credence (KREE-dentz) Shelf or table at chancel wall which holds sacramental vessels and offering plates.

crosier (KROH-zher) Crook-shaped staff often carried by a bishop in his/her own synod as a sign of shepherding authority.

crucifer The lay assisting minister or senior acolyte who carries the processional cross or crucifix.

crucifix Cross with a corpus attached.

cruet Glass vessel containing wine for the Holy Communion, oil for anointing, or water for the lavabo.

daily prayer The daily services of readings and prayer, including Morning Prayer (Matins), Evening Prayer (Vespers), and Prayer at the Close of the Day (Compline).

dalmatic (dal-MAH-tik) Eucharistic vestment sometimes worn over the alb by the principle assisting minister during festive celebrations of the Holy Communion.

dossal Fabric hanging behind and above traditional east- wall altar.

east wall The wall behind the altar, regardless of whether the wall is geographically to the east.

eastwall altar An altar attached to the wall.

Easter Principal festival of the church year which celebrates Christ's resurrection. Easter Day (which occurs between March 22 and April 25) is known as the Resurrection of Our Lord and as the "queen of feasts." The Easter season lasts for fifty days, a "week of weeks."

Easter Vigil Festive liturgy on Easter Eve which includes the lighting of the new fire and procession of the paschal candle, readings from scripture, Holy Baptism with the renewal of baptismal vows, and Holy Communion.

elements The earthly elements used in the celebration of the sacraments: bread and wine in Holy Communion, and water in Holy Baptism.

Epiphany Principal festival celebrated on January 6, marking the visit of the magi to Jesus and the consequent revelation of Christ to the world.

epistle side The right side of the altar as the congregation faces it.

eucharist (YOO-kar-ist) From the Greek for "thanksgiving"; a name for the Holy Communion. The sacrament of Word, bread, and wine (in which the two earthly elements constitute the body and blood of our Lord) for which we give thanks, and

through which we are nourished and strengthened in Christ's name and sustained in baptismal unity in him.

Evening Prayer An evening worship service of scripture readings and prayer; also known as Vespers.

ewer (YOO-er) A pitcher used for carrying water to the baptismal font.

fair linen Top white linen cloth covering the mensa of the altar and thus serving as the table cloth for the Lord's Supper.

fall Old term sometimes used for paraments on altar, pulpit, and lectern.

flagon (FLAG-un) Pitcher-like vessel from which wine is poured into the chalice for the Holy Communion.

font From the Latin for "fountain"; the pool or basin which holds water for Holy Baptism.

fraction Ceremonial breaking of the bread in the Holy Communion liturgy.

free-standing altar An altar which is not attached to the wall, and behind which the ministers stand (facing the congregation) for the celebration of Holy Communion.

frontal Parament which covers the entire front of the altar, from the top edge of the mensa down to the predella; *see also* Laudian frontal.

frontlet Narrow altar parament usually hung in pairs and extending only part way to the predella; not now commonly used.

funeral pall Large white cloth cover placed on the coffin when brought into the nave for the burial liturgy. If an urn is used for ashes, a small white cloth is used to cover it.

gold Liturgical color for Easter Day, giving special prominence to this single most important festival of the year.

Good Friday The Friday in Holy Week which observes Christ's crucifixion and death. The chancel and altar are bare of all appointments, paraments, and linens.

gospel side Left side of the altar as the congregation faces it.

gradine (grah-DEEN) From the Latin for "step"; a step or shelf at the rear of the mensa of an eastwall altar, on which cross, candlesticks, and flowers are placed. Also known as retable.

Greek cross Ancient form of the cross in which the four arms are of equal length.

green Liturgical color for the nonfestival seasons after Pentecost and Epiphany; symbolic of growth in the Christian way of life.

hearse A triangular candelabrum used for Tenebrae.

Holy Trinity The First Sunday after Pentecost, which celebrates the doctrine of the Trinity (one God in three persons: Father, Son, and Holy Spirit).

Holy Week The week between the Sunday of the Passion (Palm Sunday) and Easter, which recalls the events of the last days of Christ's life.

host Wafer, made of unleavened bread, for the Holy Communion.

host box Short, round, covered container which holds the supply of hosts for the Holy Communion. Also known as pyx.

incense Mixture of resins for ceremonial burning, symbolic of our prayers rising to God (see Psalm 141); one of the gifts of the magi to Jesus on the Epiphany.

intinction From the Latin for "to dip"; the practice of administering the eucharistic elements by dipping the host into the wine; does not work well with whole bread.

Laudian frontal A type of frontal which entirely covers the top and all sides (to the floor) of a free-standing altar.

lavabo bowl (lah-VAH-boh) Bowl used for the act of cleansing the presiding minister's hands (this act is known as the lavabo) in the Holy Communion or after the imposition of ashes or oil.

lectern Reading stand in the chancel from which the scripture readings may be proclaimed.

lectionary The appointed system of scripture readings for the days of the church year. Also refers to the book that contains these readings.

lector A lay assisting minister who reads the first and second readings from scripture in the Holy Communion liturgy, or the biblical readings in other rites.

Lent From the Anglo-Saxon for "spring"; the penitential forty-day season (excluding Sundays) before

Easter, beginning with Ash Wednesday. Symbolic of Christ's forty days in the wilderness. Lent is traditionally the season when candidates prepare for Holy Baptism, which is celebrated at the Easter Vigil.

lenten veil Cloth used to cover crosses, sculpture, pictures, and other objects during Lent.

linens Refers to three groups of white linen cloths: altar linens (cerecloth, protector linen, and fair linen), communion linens (corporal, pall, purificators, and veil), and other linens (credence linen, offertory table linen, lavabo towel, and baptismal towel).

liturgy From the Greek for "the people's work"; the prescribed worship service of the church.

lucernarium (loo-cher-NAHR-ee-um) From the Latin for "light"; the service of light at the beginning of Evening Prayer.

Magnificat (mahg-NIFF-ih-kaht) Latin title for the canticle "My soul proclaims the greatness of the Lord," which is the gospel canticle in Evening Prayer, and is from Luke 1:46-55.

Matins (MAT-ins) From the Latin for "morning"; morning service of Scripture reading and prayer; also known as Morning Prayer.

Maundy Thursday (MAWN-dee) From the Latin *mandatum* for "commandment"; the Thursday in Holy Week which commemorates the institution of the Holy Communion at the Last Supper, during which Jesus commanded his disciples to love one another.

memorial garden Usually a courtyard garden on church property in which ashes are mixed with the soil for interment after cremation.

mensa From the Latin for "table"; the top surface of the altar.

missal Altar service book.

missal stand Stand or cushion on the altar on which the altar service book is placed during the Holy Communion liturgy.

miter (MY-ter) From the Greek for "turban." A liturgical hat worn by a bishop.

Morning Prayer Morning service of Scripture reading and prayer; also known as Matins.

morse The clasp used to fasten a cope.

narthex Entrance hall and gathering space of a church building which leads to the nave.

nave From the Latin for "ship"; the section of the church building between the narthex and the chancel, where the congregation assembles for worship.

new fire The fire kindled on Easter Eve, used to light the paschal candle for the Easter Vigil. Symbolic of Christ's resurrected presence.

Nunc dimittis Latin title for the canticle from Luke 2:29-32, "Lord, now you let your servant go in peace," used in Compline and as a post-communion canticle after Holy Communion.

occasional service Liturgical rite used from time to time, including rites for burial, marriage, healing, ordination, dedication of a church building, installation of a pastor, confirmation (Affirmation of Baptism), etc.

offertory table A small table near the rear of the nave which holds the bread and wine prior to the offertory.

ordinary Those parts of the eucharistic liturgy which do not change from week to week.

orphrey (OR-free) From the Latin for "gold." Ornamental band on a chasuble or parament.

ossuary Small container holding the remains after a cremation.

pall Linen-covered square placed over rim of the chalice. (See also funeral pall.)

Palm Sunday See Sunday of the Passion.

paraments Cloth hangings of various seasonal liturgical colors used to adorn the altar and pulpit/ambo/lectern.

paschal candle Large white candle carried in procession during the Easter Vigil, placed near the altar and lighted during the Easter season, symbolizing Christ's resurrected presence. At other times of the year, it is placed near the font and lighted for Holy Baptism, and placed at the head of the coffin and lighted for the burial liturgy.

paten (PATT-en) Plate used to hold bread or hosts during the Holy Communion liturgy.

pectoral cross A cross on a chain, worn around the neck by a bishop.

Pentecost From the Greek for "fiftieth day"; principal festival of the church year, occurring fifty days after Easter. Celebrates the descent of the Holy Spirit to the crowd gathered in Jerusalem.

Phos hilaron (FOHS HILL-uh-ron) Greek for "light of glory"; hence, the Greek name for the canticle in Evening Prayer which begins "Joyous light of glory."

piscina A special drain in the sacristy which goes directly into the ground, used for disposal of baptismal water and wine remaining in the chalice after the Holy Communion.

Prayer at the Close of the Day Night prayer service used as the last worship before retiring for the night. Also known as Compline.

predella (preh-DELL-ah) Raised platform in the chancel on which the altar is placed.

presiding minister The ordained pastor who presides at a worship service.

prie-dieu (pree-DYOO) French term for "prayer desk"; used in the chancel for daily prayer services, confirmation, and weddings, as well as by ministers at other times when kneeling for prayer is desired.

processional cross A cross or crucifix on a tall staff used to lead processions.

processional torch See torch.

propers The varying portions of the eucharistic liturgy which are appointed for each day (or season) of the church year; include the prayer of the day, psalm, readings, proper verse, proper offertory, and proper preface.

protector linen White linen cloth placed on the mensa between the cerecloth and the fair linen, to which the parament may be attached.

pulpit Raised reading desk in the chancel from which the gospel is read and the sermon preached. See also ambo.

purificator Square linen napkin used to cleanse the rim of the chalice during the distribution of Holy Communion.

purple Liturgical color for Lent, symbolizing penitence. Also the alternate color for Advent, symbolizing the royal color of the coming King.

pyx (PIKS) See host box.

red Bright red liturgical color, symbolic of the fire of the Holy Spirit. Used on the Day of Pentecost, Reformation Day, martyrs' days, and on major church occasions such as ordination, the dedication of a church building, church anniversaries, and synod/churchwide assemblies.

reredos (RAIR-eh-doss) Carved stone or wood panel behind and above an eastwall altar.

Responsive Prayer Brief liturgical order of versicles and responses.

retable (REE-tay-bel) A step or shelf at the rear of the mensa of an eastwall altar, on which cross, candlesticks, and flowers are placed. Also known as a gradine.

rite The text and ceremonies of a liturgical worship service.

rubric From the Latin for "red"; a direction for the proper conduct of a worship service. Rubrics are usually printed in red.

sacrament A rite commanded by Christ that uses an earthly element with the word of God to convey God's grace; Holy Baptism and Holy Communion.

sacristy A room used for storage and preparation of items needed in worship; also used for vesting before services.

sanctuary The section of the chancel which immediately surrounds the altar.

sanctuary lamp A constantly burning candle sometimes suspended from the ceiling or mounted on the chancel wall; in Roman Catholic and some Episcopal churches, symbolizes the reserved sacrament.

scarlet The deep red liturgical color used from the Sunday of the Passion (Palm Sunday) through Maundy Thursday. Symbolic of the blood of the passion of Christ.

sedilia (seh-DEE-lee-ah) Seats in the chancel for the worship leaders.

sign of the cross Gesture of tracing the outline of the cross with the hand, as a mark of belonging to Christ in Holy Baptism (during which it is first placed on one's forehead).

spoon Perforated utensil sometimes used to remove foreign particles from wine in the chalice. A spoon is also used with the granular incense.

stole Cloth band in liturgical color worn over the alb or surplice around a pastor's neck and hanging to the knees. Signifies ordination and the yoke of obedience to Christ.

stripping of the altar Ceremony at the conclusion of the Maundy Thursday liturgy, in which all appointments, linens, and paraments are removed from the altar and chancel in preparation for Good Friday.

Sunday of the Passion The first day of Holy Week, also known as Palm Sunday. Commemorates both Christ's triumphant entry into Jerusalem and his crucifixion.

superfrontal Short parament which hangs over the front of the mensa of an eastwall altar; now rarely used.

surplice White vestment worn over the cassock; used especially for daily prayer services.

Te Deum laudamus (tay DAY-um lau-DAH-moos) Latin for "We praise you, God"; a title for the canticle used in Morning Prayer.

Tenebrae (TENN-eh-bray) From the Latin for "shadows"; a service sometimes used evenings during Holy Week, in which candles on a Tenebrae candle hearse are gradually extinguished.

thurible Vessel in which incense is burned; also known as a censer.

thurifer The person who carries the thurible.

torch Large candle on a staff carried in processions, often flanking the processional cross or gospel book.

torchbearer An acolyte who carries a processional torch.

Transfiguration Festival celebrated on the last Sunday after the Epiphany, recalling Christ's transfiguration on the mountain.

Triduum (TRIH-doo-um) Latin for "three days"; the three sacred days from Maundy Thursday evening through Easter Evening, which together celebrate the unity of the paschal mystery of Christ's death and resurrection.

tunicle Eucharistic vestment less ornate than a dalmatic; may be worn over an alb by the "junior" assisting minister at festive Holy Communion services.

urn *see* ossuary.

veil Cloth placed over sacramental vessels before and after the celebration of Holy Communion.

versicles Brief lines of scripture (often from the psalms) sung or said responsively in certain rites, including daily prayer.

Vespers From the Latin for "evening"; an evening worship service of scripture readings and prayer. Also known as Evening Prayer.

vigil A liturgical service on the eve of a festival, such as the Easter Vigil.

white Liturgical color used on festivals of Christ, the weeks of Christmas and Easter, The Holy Trinity, and certain saints' days. Symbolizes joy, gladness, purity, and the light of Christ.

FOR FURTHER HELP

Some of the following books are helpful to keep in the working sacristy for reference; others will serve also as a good basis for group study and/or devotions at altar guild meetings.

Baker, Robert J., Evelyn Kaehler, and Peter Mazar, eds. *A Lent Sourcebook* (two volumes). Chicago: Liturgy Training Publications, 1990. A collection of readings, meditations, and prayers related to Ash Wednesday and the season of Lent. Useful for devotions at meetings.

Bangert, Mark P. *Symbols and Terms of the Church.* Minneapolis: Augsburg Fortress, 1990. Illustrations and explanations of 75 basic Christian symbols.

Brand, Eugene L., and S. Anita Stauffer. *By Water and the Spirit.* Philadelphia: Parish Life Press, 1979. An illustrated introduction to the liturgy for Holy Baptism in *Lutheran Book of Worship.* Good for study sessions.

Dornheim, John F. C. *And He Took a Loaf of Bread.* Fulton, Maryland: Campanile Press, 1998. Extensive collection of eucharistic bread recipes, along with commentary on the meaning and use of altar bread.

Halmo, Joan, and Frank Henderson, compilers. *A Triduum Sourcebook* (three volumes). Chicago: Liturgy Training Publications, 1996. A collection of readings, meditations, and prayers related to the Three Days: Maundy Thursday through Easter Sunday. Useful for devotions at meetings.

Harter, Joyce, and Lucy Brusic. *Weaving for Worship.* McMinnville, Oregon: 1998. Practical illustrated guide for handweaving of vestments, paraments, and textile art for churches and synagogues.

Huck, Gabe. *The Three Days.* Revised edition. Chicago: Liturgy Training Publications, 1992. Includes helpful practical instructions for making Paschal/Easter candles and baptismal garments.

Huffman, Walter, and S. Anita Stauffer. *Where We Worship.* Minneapolis: Augsburg Publishing House; Philadelphia: LCA Board of Publication; and St. Louis: Concordia Publishing House, 1987. Basic illustrated introduction to the worship space, along with process guide by R. R. Van Loon for congregations considering renovation or a new building.

Joseph, Elizabeth. *Sewing Church Linens.* Harrisburg, PA: Morehouse Publishing, 1991. Practical guide for making and caring for linens for liturgical use.

Lathrop, Gordon W. *Living Witnesses: The Adult Catechumenate*. Winnipeg: Evangelical Lutheran Church in Canada, 1992. Rites for the process of preparing and baptizing youth and adults for Holy Baptism.

Marchal, Michael G., and Rosemary G. Conrad. "Womb and Tomb and Bath: A Temporary Baptismal Pool." *Catechumenate*, January 1989. Instructions for easily constructing a temporary pool for baptismal immersion of adults, especially at the Easter Vigil.

Mazar, Peter. *To Crown the Year*. Chicago: Liturgy Training Publications, 1995. A practical guide to decorating the interior and exterior of the church for the liturgical year.

Mori, Joyce. *Crosses of Many Cultures*. Harrisburg, PA: Morehouse, 1998. Designs for applique.

O'Gorman, Thomas J., ed. *An Advent Sourcebook*. Chicago: Liturgy Training Publications, 1988. A collection of readings, meditations, and prayers related to the season of Advent. Useful for devotions at meetings.

Pfatteicher, Philip H. *Commentary on the Lutheran Book of Worship*. Minneapolis: Augsburg Fortress, 1990. A commentary on the liturgies and calendar of the *LBW*. Helpful for study at meetings.

_____. *Commentary on the Occasional Services*. Philadelphia: Fortress Press, 1983. A commentary on the rites in Occasional Services. Helpful for study at meetings.

_____. *Festivals and Commemorations*. Minneapolis: Augsburg, 1980. A handbook to the calendar of festivals and commemorations in *LBW*, useful for study or devotions at meetings.

Philippart, David. *Clothed in Glory: Vesting the Church*. Chicago: Liturgy Training Publications, 1997. Beautifully illustrated, practical guide to linens, paraments, vestments, baptismal garments, funeral palls, banners and other hangings.

Ramshaw, Gail. *A Metaphorical God*. Chicago: Liturgy Training Publications, 1995. Excellent book for devotions at meetings, or as a basis for some study sessions. Previously published as *Letters for God's Name*.

Ramshaw, Gail, and Lathrop, Gordon, eds. *Psalter for the Christian People*. Collegeville, Minnesota: Liturgical Press, 1993. Emended version of the psalter in *Lutheran Book of Worship* and *Book of Common Prayer*.

Readings and Prayers: The Revised Common Lectionary. Minneapolis: Augsburg Fortress, 1995. Booklet listing the appointed lessons and prayers for each Sunday; helpful in understanding the thrust of each day in order to prepare and decorate appropriately.

Simcoe, Mary Ann, ed. *A Christmas Sourcebook*. Chicago: Liturgy Training Publications, 1984. A collection of readings, meditations, and prayers related to Christmas and Epiphany. Useful for devotions at meetings.

Spencer, Frances Kipps. *Chrismons: Basic Series,* third ed. Danville, Virginia: Lutheran Church of the Ascension, 1972.

_____. *Chrismons: Advanced Series,* second ed. Danville, Virginia: Lutheran Church of the Ascension, 1993.

Stauffer, S. Anita. "Contemporary Questions on Church Architecture and Culture," in Stauffer, S. Anita, ed., *Worship and Culture in Dialogue.* Geneva, Switzerland: Lutheran World Federation, 1994. Practical essay on how church art and architecture relate to various cultural traditions. Useful for study at meetings.

_____. *On Baptismal Fonts: Ancient and Modern.* Cambridge, England: Grove Books, 1994. Illustrated guide to the meaning, design, placement, and use of baptismal fonts/pools.

_____. *Re-examining Baptismal Fonts.* Collegeville, MN: Liturgical Press, 1991. Videotape about the meaning of baptism and the design of fonts which enable the meaning to be enacted.

Stulken, Marilyn Kay. *Hymnal Companion to the Lutheran Book of Worship.* Philadelphia: Fortress, 1981. *With One Voice Reference Companion.* Minneapolis: Augsburg Fortress, 2000. Background information on the texts and tunes of all of the hymns in *LBW* and *WOV*.

Sundays and Seasons. Minneapolis: Augsburg Fortress. An annual guide to Sunday and festival worship in the Lutheran context, including suggestions for decorating the worship space.

Taylor, Jean. *Flowers in Church.* Harrisburg: Morehouse, 1976. Practical guide for planning and arranging flowers for a wide variety of liturgical occasions.

Use of the Means of Grace, The: A Statement on the Practice of Word and Sacrament. Adopted for guidance and practice by the Fifth Biennial Churchwide Assembly of the Evangelical Lutheran Church in America, August 19, 1997.

Van Loon, R. R., and S. Anita Stauffer. *Worship Wordbook.* Minneapolis: Augsburg Fortress, 1995. A practical and comprehensive guide to terms used in liturgical worship, providing not only definitions and background information, but also guidelines for usage.

Current Service Books

(Listed in chronological order)

Lutheran Book of Worship (LBW). Minneapolis and Philadelphia: Augsburg Publishing House and Lutheran Church in America Board of Publication, 1978. Basic liturgy book and hymnal for Lutheran congregations.

Lutheran Book of Worship–Ministers Edition. Minneapolis and Philadelphia: Augsburg Publishing House and Lutheran Church in America Board of Publication, 1978. The *LBW* altar book (also available in a smaller desk edition for reference use) containing complete rubrics, calendar details, and propers.

Occasional Services. Minneapolis and Philadelphia: Augsburg Publishing House and Lutheran Church in America Board of Publication, 1982. A companion to the *LBW*, containing rites for ordination, installations, dedications and blessings, marriage, burial, the ministry of healing, and other occasional services.

With One Voice (WOV). Minneapolis: Augsburg Fortress, 1995. Supplemental Lutheran resource for liturgy and hymns. Also available in a Leaders Edition with additional liturgical texts and notes on the liturgy (but no hymns).

Welcome to Christ: Lutheran Rites for the Catechumenate. Minneapolis: Augsburg Fortress, 1997. Rites for preparing for and celebrating the baptism of youth and adults. Three booklets of background, practical guidance, and the rites themselves for the adult catechumenate.

Libro de Liturgia y Cántico. Minneapolis: Augsburg Fortress, 1998. Hispanic Lutheran liturgy book and hymnal.

This Far by Faith. Minneapolis: Augsburg Fortress, 1999. African American Lutheran liturgy and hymn supplement.

LECTIONARY

Lectionary for Worship: Revised Common Lectionary (three volumes: cycle A, cycle B, cycle C; also available in a one-volume hardbound ritual edition). Minneapolis: Augsburg Fortress, 1995–97. Contains complete texts of the appointed readings, in the New Revised Standard Version (NRSV) translation.

ECCLESIASTICAL SUPPLIERS

Ashby Company
P. O. Box 2051
Erie, PA 16512
800-413-2220
www.ashbypublishing.com

Meyer-Vogelpohl
717 Race Street
Cincinnati, OH 45202
800-543-0264
www.mvchurchgoods.com

Augsburg Fortress
P. O. Box 1209
Minneapolis, MN 55440-1209
800-328-4648
www.augsburgfortress.org

INDEX